Big Picture RSHE is accompanied by a number of printable online materials, designed to ensure this resource best supports your professional needs

Go to https://resourcecentre.routledge.com/speechmark and click on the cover of this book

Answer the question prompt using your copy of the book to gain access to the online content.

"*Big Picture RSHE* is a very clear, empowering and comprehensive set of resources. They are rooted in high-quality research, practical teaching and an educational philosophy that prepares and educates children very well indeed."

Naomi Leaver, *Executive Headteacher,*
Robinsfield George Eliot Federation Westminster London

"This really is a superb resource for primary schools. *Big Picture RSHE* is easy to read and use – clearly identifying the topics that are being covered, with detail that is thorough and manageable and with the added flexibility to introduce, consolidate or assess knowledge. The structure of the toolkits gives the children familiarity and a route to fully deepen their understanding of the topic. The resource has been created in a fun, sensitive way and the use of analogies is brilliant, making it accessible and relatable to children. It will undoubtedly promote discussion and participation in the classroom."

Natalie Brown, *Assistant Head, Pastoral and PSHEE Lead,*
Hilden Grange School Tonbridge

Big Picture RSHE

How are families like trees? How are children like caterpillars?

Containing age-appropriate analogies for key Relationships, Sex and Health Education topics, this book provides carefully constructed, memorable metaphors for teaching some of the trickiest concepts around relationships and sexual development.

Each toolkit opens with a story that draws comparisons between a common childhood experience and a conceptual RSHE topic. Learners are supported in breaking down the analogy, comparing each part of the familiar story to a new concept. Knowledge is deepened with matching games, extension activities and teaching tips.

The book includes:

- Ready-made toolkits for the classroom

- Printable activities to engage learners

- Cross-curricular extension activities within each toolkit to support and enhance lesson plans

- Clear teaching notes with advice for inclusive and accessible delivery that considers learners' lived experiences

Crafted by RSHE experts, this off-the-shelf resource offers RSHE teachers, PSHE departments and other educators a thread of consistency across curricula to deliver a seamless learning experience in Key Stage Two and beyond. These skillfully crafted and age-appropriate metaphors are the perfect way to neutralise awkwardness, engage cross-curricular thinking and make learning stick.

Sophie Manning is an impact investor and CEO coach, helping charity leaders to move the needle on social injustice in the UK. She is the parent of two young boys and co-author of *Sex Ed on the Cards*, a game which aims to change the conversation around sex, bodies, consent and relationships.

Yoan Reed is an independent RSE consultant with more than 25 years of experience working in the field of Sexual and Reproductive Health Rights and Comprehensive Sexuality Education both domestically and internationally. She is the founder of Teaching Lifeskills, providing RSE and training in educational settings and the co-founder of Outspoken Sex Ed, a CIC promoting parental engagement in RSE.

Big Picture RSHE

Ready-Made Analogies and Practical Activities for Relationships, Sex and Health Education in the Primary Classroom

Sophie Manning and Yoan Reed

Routledge
Taylor & Francis Group

LONDON AND NEW YORK

Designed cover image: Jon Jacks

First published 2024
by Routledge
4 Park Square, Milton Park, Abingdon, Oxon OX14 4RN

and by Routledge
605 Third Avenue, New York, NY 10158

Routledge is an imprint of the Taylor & Francis Group, an informa business

British Library Cataloguing-in-Publication Data
A catalogue record for this book is available from the British Library

ISBN: 9781032489667 (hbk)
ISBN: 9781032489650 (pbk)
ISBN: 9781003391654 (ebk)

DOI: 10.4324/9781003391654

Typeset in DIN Schriften
by Deanta Global Publishing Services, Chennai, India

Access the Support Material: https://resourcecentre.routledge.com/speechmark

Contents

Contents

Section 1

About this resource and its context

DOI: 10.4324/9781003391654-1

High quality Relationships, Sex and Health Education (RSHE) depends on unbiased guidance by skilled educators delivered in a safe environment. Children need to learn the facts, express their own lived experiences and explore attitudes and values. *Big Picture RSHE* supports engaging and experiential learning while facilitating the many elements of effective and safe RSHE.

A. What is Relationships, Sex and Health Education (RSHE) at primary level?

All children and young people deserve to be prepared for adult life with an age-appropriate understanding of healthy relationships and intimacy. Best practice in RSHE at primary level follows a spiral curriculum, which provides a foundation for learning that can be extended into secondary school and beyond.

In primary school, RSHE mainly focuses on

- healthy and respectful relationships.
- learning about children's developing bodies (particularly puberty changes).
- staying safe, including knowing where to find help and support.

B. What is *Big Picture RSHE*?

Big Picture RSHE is a teaching resource designed to support educators of primary-aged children – in particular those aged 9–11 (and beyond, where appropriate).

It uses analogy, which is a recognised tool in the teaching of new concepts (see Section E: How do analogies support learning in RSHE), to

1. **introduce, consolidate or evaluate understanding** of core RSHE themes.
2. **improve and diversify** the delivery of RSHE.

The resource contains 15 ready-made toolkits that educators can copy, adapt and deliver.

Each toolkit offers a hands-on 30- to 60-minute activity that provides a thread of consistency to tie together an existing RSHE curriculum and scheme of work.

C. Why use *Big Picture RSHE*?

Some RSHE themes can be sensitive to teach – so how can we avoid 'death by worksheet' and bring them to life in an accessible way? *Big Picture RSHE* is a resource that:

Neutralises awkwardness in RSHE It takes the sting out of some of the trickiest topics in the RSHE curriculum, using analogy to land important but hard-to-teach knowledge, and helps to begin a dialogue around values.	**Makes learning stick** It fixes learning in children's minds by equipping learners of all styles (e.g. auditory or visual) with deep-rooted, memorable mental images.	**Supports evidence of learning for school inspections** It offers a way to deepen and consolidate understanding *and* doubles as a method for baseline, formative and summative assessments of learning.
Reflects best practice It shoulders any considerations of what is age-and stage-appropriate learning in RHSE.	**Crosses subject boundaries** It supports a seamless learning experience utilising concepts from children's everyday lives, engaging storytelling, metaphor and logic to build literary, scientific and philosophical thinking.	**Is inclusive** Its content and reach embrace everyday lived experiences and diversity in its many forms. This supports learning in which every child, their family background and community is reflected and respected.

D. Who is this resource for?

This resource is developed for primary school teachers, Personal Social Health Education (PSHE) and Relationships and Sex Education (RSE) subject leads, pastoral staff and parents/carers. It is also suitable for other professionals working with children and young people. such as youth workers, social workers, residential and activity facilitators and anyone else interested in engaging children with the big picture of RSHE. As different professionals and adults will find this resource useful when taking a lead in RSHE, we refer to these responsible adults collectively as 'educators.'

E. How do analogies support learning in RSHE?

An analogy compares one thing with another in order to clarify or facilitate understanding. In education, analogies help learners to apply their own prior knowledge to grasp an abstract concept or retain new information.

Analogical reasoning and relational thinking are part of everyday learning both in- and outside of the classroom. The analogies in this resource mimic that everyday process – using similes and metaphors to draw comparisons between RSHE concepts and accessible ideas drawn from daily life.

Analogies have a *source* (the object or concept already familiar to the learner) and a *target* (the object or concept to which existing knowledge is transferred).[1] For example, in the **Changing Bodies** toolkit within this resource, the *source* is a **caterpillar**, and the *target* is **children's bodies**. Children will be supported in drawing comparisons between the two. The caterpillar metaphor supports learners to draw the inference that it is normal for children, like caterpillars, to change when they turn into grown-ups.

SOURCE	THE LEARNING PROCESS	TARGET
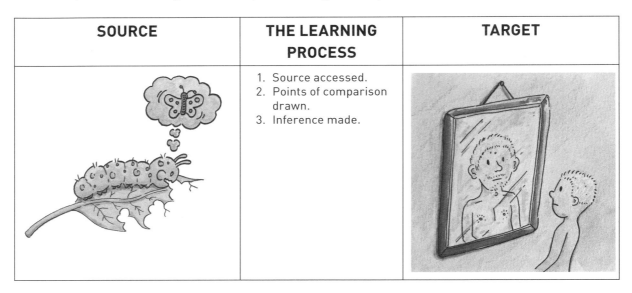	1. Source accessed. 2. Points of comparison drawn. 3. Inference made.	

Analogies work best when they are formulated – as in this toolkit – to[2]

- minimise distractions within the source.
- clearly identify both the source and the target used in the analogy.
- use storytelling and visual representations.
- use prompts to support the comparison process.
- provide cues and relational language to deepen conceptual understanding.

Analogies are an effective way to introduce and consolidate RSHE themes in particular because they

---

1 Gentner, D., 1983. Structure-mapping: A theoretical framework for analogy. *Cognitive Science*, 7(2), pp. 155–170.
2 Vendetti, M.S., Matlen, B.J., Richland, L.E. and Bunge, S.A., 2015. Analogical reasoning in the classroom: Insights from cognitive science. *Mind, Brain, and Education*, 9(2), pp. 100–106.

- **neutralise taboos.** Children's feelings of awkwardness when faced with taboo topics such as sex and bodies can lead to behaviour that interferes with teaching. Use of everyday analogies can help bypass this disruption.
- **help with abstract concepts.** Often, RSHE includes information that can be actively mystified or withheld from children, such as how a baby is made and the correct terminology for the private body parts, meaning that they haven't built up a grounding in the topic through repeat exposure. Everyday analogies offer a shortcut to this familiarity.

F. Is the resource relevant in my context?

Because RSHE themes are universal to all learners, *Big Picture RSHE* is relatable to a broad educational context that focuses on children's social and emotional development as well as mental health and physical well-being. Whatever your context, make sure you align your approach to your setting's safeguarding, equality, anti-bullying, behaviour and online safety policies.

All educational settings should have a clear and transparent RSHE policy which defines sex education to clarify what part of the RSHE curriculum contains elements of sex education.

This resource clearly identifies which toolkits we believe to be part of sex education, drawing on the Sex Education Forum's RSHE definition guidance.[3] You are encouraged to refer to working policies and definitions of sex education within your own setting to ensure alignment with the distinctions made in the toolkits.

3 Sex Education Forum, 2020. RSE definitions guide. https://www.sexeducationforum.org.uk/.

Section 2

How to use this resource

DOI: 10.4324/9781003391654-2

A. How do I use the toolkits?

We have structured each toolkit to first deliver a central analogy and second to draw inferences and deepen children's understanding of the corresponding RSHE topic.

1. **PART 1: THE STORY** – A story to be read aloud along with prompting questions, laying the foundations for the activity.
2. **PART 2: THE COMPARISON ACTIVITY** – A discussion sheet (to be photocopied) to support learners to draw comparisons between the story and the RSHE topic that sits alongside it.
3. **PART 3: THE MATCHING ACTIVITY** – A set of "matching cards" (to be photocopied) helps learners to unpack the metaphor and deepen their understanding. This part also includes extension activities to support learning.

This resource adopts a thematic rather than a chronological approach. This gives users the flexibility to pick toolkits that are relevant to their RSHE curriculum and chosen scheme of work.

The toolkits can be used in a variety of ways:

- to **introduce** a new concept and new knowledge,
- to **consolidate** learning from RSHE lessons,
- in **assessment** – baseline, formative and summative assessment of learning.

Practice example 1: Assessing learning needs	Practice example 2: Addressing an issue
Before teaching a scheme of work on puberty, you choose the toolkit **"Changing Bodies"** to assess learning needs. The output from Part 2 (the comparison activity) works as a baseline assessment and tells you where there are gaps in knowledge. You revisit the toolkit after you have completed a unit of work on puberty and use the output from Part 3 (the matching activity) to assess formative or summative learning and remind the class of the key concepts.	You have become aware of inappropriate and sexist language used among a group of learners. To start addressing the issue within the class you choose the toolkit **"Respecting all genders,"** including a reflection activity that applies learning from the session to make changes in classroom behaviour. You share your observations with colleagues and parents. You then pick an extension activity from the toolkit and ask groups to share their learning in a dedicated assembly.

Practice example 3: Consolidating learning	Practice example 4: Supporting SEND and inclusion
You recently delivered a session on puberty changes, and at the end of the session, a group of children asked a question about wet dreams. You didn't feel quite prepared for the question but answered as best as you could. On reflection, you are unsure if you managed to give comprehensive and accurate information. You decide to use the toolkit "**Wet Dreams**" to expand on and consolidate the learning the children received previously and to address and discuss the theme in more detail.	There is a child in your class with learning difficulties who is from an ethnic minority group and lives with their grandparents. You plan to use the "**Families**" toolkit, and you consider how the child is supported to follow the analogy and what you need to be aware of to make them feel included and visible when exploring the central theme of family composition. You discuss the needs of the child with their family and your Designated Safeguarding Lead and check your setting's special educational needs and disabilities (SEND) and Inclusion policies before delivering the session.

B. Things to consider when using this resource

Engaging parents/carers in RSHE

Parents are recognised as their child's primary relationships and sex educator. School–home communication around RSHE is an important element of developing children's learning at home. The following are suggestions on how you can support parents in their RSHE role.

- If parents show an interest or have questions about RSHE, you should signpost them to an accessible and transparent RSHE policy and help them understand the related curriculum and schemes of work. This is particularly important if parents ask for their child to be withdrawn from sex education elements of RSHE.
- Organise a parent session and engage them in a couple of the toolkits within this resource so that they can experience how and what the children are learning. Often, parental concerns are alleviated when they understand RSHE better and see the resources that are used in class.

Space, time and competencies for RSHE at primary

Teaching RSHE requires an enthusiastic, interactive and learner-centred approach. Educators of RSHE need to feel supported and valued and have access to opportunities for developing the competencies that are paramount for good quality and effective RSHE: knowledge, skills and attitudes.[1]

To make the RSHE you deliver meaningful and effective, think about the following:

- respond to the needs of the learners;
- plan and structure curriculum time;
- access adequate support, training and continuous professional development (CPD) opportunities;
- address your competencies – knowledge, skills and attitudes;
- be aware of inclusion and safeguarding measures.

Using this resource within the context of an inclusive curriculum

Every educational setting is unique, and all educators face the challenge of differentiating the approach to make it age, stage and culturally appropriate while observing guidance requirements and meeting children's specific needs.

RSHE should be delivered in a non-discriminatory and non-judgmental way to ensure all children feel included in the learning environment and see their own lives reflected within the content of learning. When using the toolkits, it is recommended that you:

- Refer to legislation and guidance around protected characteristics to promote equality and challenge discrimination of any kind.
- Consult your setting's RSHE, Special Educational Needs and Disabilities (SEND), safeguarding, anti-bullying, behaviour, and other relevant policies to frame the approach when using the toolkits.
- Consider the make-up of the groups of learners and take into account their age, maturity, abilities, cultural and social contexts when planning activities, as these all impact the learners' lived experiences, learning needs and their thinking. Be mindful of intersectionality; you may have learners with more than one differentiation.
- Challenge assumptions and misconceptions in group discussions to ensure that all learners feel included, respected and represented.

---

1 World Health Organization (2017). Training matters: A framework for core competencies of sexuality educators. https://www.bzga-whocc.de/en/publications/concepts/training-matters-a-framework/.

Special educational needs and disabilities (SEND)

Children with SEND have the same right as their peers to access good quality and comprehensive RSHE that meets their needs. In fact, because children with SEND are also more vulnerable to bullying, exploitation and abuse, learning on topics such as 'healthy relationships' is an important safeguarding measure.

For some children with SEND, symbolic and abstract explanations will be challenging. Although this resource is not specifically designed for SEND learners, it uses storytelling, visuals, prompts, discussion cards and keywords that will help make it accessible to some SEND learners. You will still need to assess individual learning needs for further support. Consult your setting's SEND policy and speak with your setting's Designated Safeguarding Lead and Special Educational Needs Coordinator (SENCo) to plan for individual children's learning.

Safeguarding

Many themes within RSHE, such as learning about healthy relationships, boundaries and correct terminology for private body parts, are safeguarding measures to help children look after themselves and others. The nature of RSHE themes can also prompt disclosure or raise concern for a child's safety and wellbeing. To ensure you and the children have a safe and comfortable learning environment that supports the management of disclosures or concerns, you must be familiar with

- creating and maintaining a comfortable, safe, inclusive and enabling learning environment – which includes agreeing a set of ground rules for RSHE sessions;
- the safeguarding and child protection policies, procedures and processes in your setting, including referral to the Designated Safeguarding Lead.

C. Step-by-step guide to using the toolkits

Before you start

1. Prepare to deliver the toolkit.
    - Read the analogy and familiarise yourself with the **learning theme** it addresses and the related **key words**.
    - Decide whether your learners have the required baseline knowledge (some toolkits assume a higher level of prior understanding).

- Use the information under "Section B: Things to consider when using this resource" (above) and the **teaching notes** within the individual toolkit to reflect on the particular needs of the group.

Introducing the activity

2. Start your session by establishing ground rules for learning in RSHE.
3. Explain metaphors using a simple example if you are using the toolkit for the first time with a group of learners.

Part 1: THE STORY

4. Read the story out aloud. Getting into character and using your tone of voice to amplify significant events and emotions will help bring the metaphor to life. Ask the **prompt questions** to start the relational learning process and take suggestions from the group of learners.

Part 2: THE COMPARISON ACTIVITY

5. Divide learners into smaller groups and hand out a photocopy of the **Comparison Activity** (A3 size recommended). Ask them to fill in the ways in which the source metaphor (e.g., different types of trees) is like the target (e.g., different types of families). Depending on the chosen toolkit and the learners' level of knowledge, groups may need support with the comparison process.

6. Take feedback from the groups and use the answer sheet to make sure learners have understood the meaning of the story. Use the **Learning Points** to reinforce that meaning. If you are using the toolkit as an assessment, gather the sheets and check levels of learning against **learning themes** and **key words**.

Part 3: THE MATCHING ACTIVITY

7. Hand out photocopies of the **Matching Activity** to the groups (A3 size is recommended). Ask learners to match up
   - the **story cards** (which explain messages about the source metaphor, e.g., different types of trees)
   - with the **explanation cards** (which explain the messages that the source metaphor reveals about the target, e.g., different types of families).

You can do this in one of two ways: EITHER cut out each box and ask the groups to physically match up the story cards with the explanation cards OR ask them to write their answers at the bottom of the sheet.

8. Take feedback from the groups and explore similarities and differences (refer to the list of **key words**). Clarify understanding and address misconceptions and misinformation. Make a note of discussion points on an interactive whiteboard or flipchart to support the reflection activity.

Following the activity

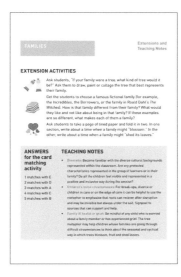

9. Use the **extension activities** if you want to
   - add a cross-curricular element,
   - address areas that need particular attention or clarification,
   - challenge more able learners.

10. Engage the learners in a reflection activity (refer to the list of **key words** and notes taken from discussion). For example:
    - Which part of the activity did you enjoy the most?
    - Which part of the story have you learned the most from?
    - How can you use the learning to teach others?
    - What do you know now that you didn't know before?
    - If you did the activity again, what would you like to learn?

11. Gather the resources and keep the activity sheets to
    - refer back to your RSHE scheme of work and level of assessment,
    - plan your next steps,
    - document and monitor learning,
    - share with colleagues/parents.

Section 3

What topics are included?

DOI: 10.4324/9781003391654-3

What topics are included?

The matrix includes

- **key icons** to indicate when learning themes in the toolkits relate to relationships education, health education, sex education and/or science –

- **learning themes** are the knowledge and understanding that each toolkit is intended to deliver; they are written in clear and age-appropriate language to enable you to communicate these points during the session;
- **the metaphor** and how it supports learning;
- **key words** (repeated in the toolkits) that help you prepare your lesson planning and guide the activity discussions.

1) FAMILIES – *Families and people who care for me*		
LEARNING THEMES	**THE METAPHOR AND HOW IT SUPPORTS LEARNING**	**KEY WORDS**
Families provide security and stability. In a healthy family people show love, care and commitment to each other. **Families come in all shapes and sizes and may have different structures.** **Losing or gaining family members is a natural part of life.** **Each family have their own unique culture and background, and each should be respected.** **Families always change and can go through difficult times.**	**"Families are like trees":** • like trees, each family can look very different; • like trees, families can be big or small; • like trees, families can offer shelter and stability; • like each part of a tree, family members each bear different responsibilities; • like trees, it is natural for families to change, shrink and grow.	Love Care Security Stability Protection Responsibility Diverse Single parent Extended Carer LGBT+ Adoption Fostering Young carers Marriage Stable relationship Separation Divorce Break-up Birth Death Support Help

R
Relationships
education

2) FRIENDSHIPS – *Healthy friendships*		
LEARNING THEMES	THE METAPHOR AND HOW IT SUPPORTS LEARNING	KEY WORDS
Healthy friendships make us feel happy and secure. **Friendships need to be nurtured with respect, honesty, care and loyalty.** **Friendships can change with time and can have ups and downs.** **Good friends show each other respect and honesty even when they disagree or have a fallout.** **When people experience unhealthy friendships, they can get support from people they trust to stand up for themselves and change the relationship.**	**"Friendships are like books":** • like books, friends can make you feel happy and secure; • like books, you need to treat friendships with care, but they can survive a bit of wear and tear; • like books, you don't need to stick to just one friend; • like books, you can take a break from a friendship and come back to it; • like books, if a friendship doesn't suit you, it's ok to stop.	Respect Truthfulness Care Trust Loyalty Kindness Generosity Inclusive Conflict Fallout Communication Mental wellbeing Support Help

R
Relationships
education

3) RESPECTING DIFFERENCE – *Diversity*		
LEARNING THEMES	**THE METAPHOR AND HOW IT SUPPORTS LEARNING**	**KEY WORDS**
There are lots of similarities and differences between people: how they look and their character, personality, preferences, culture and background. **Other people may be different but showing respect and treating them as equals will make us learn and appreciate new things.** **We often have more in common than meets the eye.** **When we communicate well and show curiosity, we can focus on similarities rather than differences.**	**"Different people are like new foods":** • like new foods, the world has many different cultures; • like new foods, if someone's culture is different from yours, that doesn't mean it's wrong; • like new foods, you might have mixed feelings about those differences, but you need to be respectful; • a curious attitude to new things will make it more interesting and fun.	Similar Different Equal Stereotype Respect Diversity Attitude Curiosity Courtesy Manners Choices Preferences Beliefs Culture LGBT+ Gender Ability Age Race/Ethnicity Discrimination Prejudice Racism Bullying Support Help

R
Relationships education

4) MAKING FRIENDS ONLINE – *Digital relationships*		
LEARNING THEMES	**THE METAPHOR AND HOW IT SUPPORTS LEARNING**	**KEY WORDS**
Making friends online can be fun and a good opportunity to learn about new things. **There are risks to making friends online when you don't know them in real life, including meeting people who want to take advantage of you, harm you or steal your personal information.** **There are tools, techniques and software that can help keep children safe when interacting with others online.** **Online safety also includes recognising when a friendship is healthy and being critical of shared information.** **Just like with face-to-face friendships, it's important to know where to go for help and support.**	**"Online friendships are like rock climbing":** • like rock climbing, online friendships can be a fun way to pass the time and can expand your horizons; • like rock climbing, you can get hurt making new friends online; you need safety equipment and training in order to do it safely; • like rock climbing, when talking to friends online, someone trustworthy needs to be ready to help.	Online behaviour Devices Social media Positive/Negative Connecting Accepting (a request) Sharing Friends Strangers Personal Privacy Information Face-to-face Anonymous Safety Risk Harassment Bullying Trolling Mental health Physical health Report Support Help

R
Relationships
education

5) WHAT YOU FIND ONLINE – *Appropriate online content*		
LEARNING THEMES	THE METAPHOR AND HOW IT SUPPORTS LEARNING	KEY WORDS
The internet is a great source of information and entertainment. It is very popular, and some use it more than others. Knowing how to manage time online is part of mental health and wellbeing. Some online platforms and sites come with age restrictions to keep people safe from inappropriate content. We might come across inappropriate content because of being curious, unaware or pressured by another person; it is not always deliberate. It is important to know how to deal with inappropriate content such as blocking, reporting and finding support and help to talk things through.	"The internet is like sweet treats": • like sweet treats, the internet is popular – it feels like it's everywhere; • as with sweets, you can't always trust your senses to tell you what's good for you online; • like sweet treats, harmful online content doesn't always come with a health warning, even though it can make you feel bad or wrong; • grown-ups can help you set limits and support you when you're not sure.	Appropriate/ Inappropriate Harmful content Safety Risk Age restrictions Curiosity Pressure Sexualised imagery/ Pornography Mental health Block Report Support Help

R
Relationships
education

6) RESPECTING ALL GENDERS – *Gender equality*

LEARNING THEMES	THE METAPHOR AND HOW IT SUPPORTS LEARNING	KEY WORDS
Gender equality means that everyone has the same rights and opportunities. People have the right to feel safe and be treated with respect and equality, no matter their sex or gender. We may look and feel different from others, but if you look closely and communicate respectfully, you'll see that people have more similarities than differences. Sexism is prejudice or discrimination based on sex or gender. We have laws and rules to protect against gender-based discrimination, bullying, harassment, abuse and violence. If a game or joke is always targeted at one gender, that is sexism. Bystander intervention is when each of us can challenge and/or report any disrespect when we see it.	**"Gender is like maths":** • like percentages, fractions and decimals in maths, all genders are equal, even if not everybody knows it; • as in maths, imbalance and inequality can be a problem that needs to be resolved; • when one group is targeted or bullied, that can often be expressed as a joke – these jokes may be common, but they are not harmless; • it's right to "solve" that problem by checking our own behaviour and calling others out.	Gender Expectations Stereotypes Equality Similarity Difference LGBT+ Choices Beliefs Culture Healthy relationships Respect Communication Power Oppression Discrimination Sexism Bullying Harassment Abuse Violence Report Support Help

7) SECRET OR SURPRISE – *Voicing concerns*		
LEARNING THEMES	**THE METAPHOR AND HOW IT SUPPORTS LEARNING**	**KEY WORDS**
Knowing the difference between planning a nice surprise and keeping a secret is important for personal safety and wellbeing. **You should trust your gut feeling when you're asked to keep something secret. If something doesn't feel right and you're worried or feel unsafe, you should ask for support and help.** **Everyone has the right to their own personal boundaries and privacy.** **Nobody should be made to feel guilty or shameful.**	**"A secret is like a backpack":** • as with a backpack, you can't tell what someone's carrying in their mind just by looking; • like a backpack, a secret can feel heavier the longer you carry it; • like a backpack, no one should have to carry a secret on their own – we can all ask to share the load; • as with a backpack, no one should be angry if you ask for help with a secret.	Secret vs. surprise Healthy/Unhealthy relationships Personal boundaries Consent Safety Privacy Choice Rights Autonomy Communication Emotions Concerns Worries Gut feeling Pressure Shame Guilt Support Help

8) CHOOSING FOR MY BODY – *Boundaries*

LEARNING THEMES	THE METAPHOR AND HOW IT SUPPORTS LEARNING	KEY WORDS
Bodily autonomy means knowing that your body belongs to you and that everyone gets to decide about their body for themselves. **You should trust your gut feeling when something doesn't feel right and know where to go to ask for help when you're worried or feel unsafe.** **Everyone has the right to their own personal boundaries and privacy.** **Nobody should be made to feel guilty or shameful.**	**"Choosing for your body is like being at a theme park":** • like waiting in the queue for a rollercoaster, what you feel can be confusing; • like going on a rollercoaster together, pressure from other people might affect your decisions about your body; • like the choices at a theme park, everybody gets to choose about their body for themselves; • like choosing not to go on a rollercoaster, nobody should make you feel bad for any decision you make about your body: you can stop or say no; • like at a theme park, you should trust your feelings and speak up.	Bodily autonomy Personal boundaries Consent Choice Rights Safety Privacy Emotions Concerns Worries Gut feeling Pressure Shame Guilt Report Support Help

9) MY AMAZING BODY – *Private body parts*		
LEARNING THEMES	**THE METAPHOR AND HOW IT SUPPORTS LEARNING**	**KEY WORDS**
Bodily autonomy means knowing that your body belongs to you and that everyone gets to decide about their body for themselves. **Knowing the vocabulary for private body parts means that you're able to have bodily autonomy and ask for support and help when you need it.** **Using correct terminology about body parts helps safeguard against ill health and abuse.** **We can all appreciate our amazing bodies for what they can do. Nothing about our bodies needs to be shameful.**	**"My body is like a computer":** • like a computer, my body it's amazing – it works like magic; • like a computer, my body needs to be treated carefully; • like a computer, my body has lots of parts with tricky names – inside and out; • like a computer, the way my body looks doesn't matter as much as what it can do; • like a computer, nobody gets to touch it unless I say they can; • like a computer, my body might be personal, but it's not a dark secret.	Bodily autonomy Boundaries Rights Safety Privacy **Correct terminology:** *Female*: Vulva, vagina, clitoris, labia *Male*: Penis, glans, foreskin, testicles, scrotum Taboo Worries Concerns Gut feeling Report Support Help

10) CHANGING BODIES – *Puberty*		
LEARNING THEMES	**THE METAPHOR AND HOW IT SUPPORTS LEARNING**	**KEY WORDS**
Puberty is the stage in life when children start to develop into adults. **It is important to know about puberty changes before they happen.** **Puberty is a normal and healthy part of life with many different emotional, physical and social changes.** **Although some puberty changes can feel strange or unsettling, it is an exciting time when we learn more about ourselves and others and become more independent.** **Having people around you who you trust and knowing where to ask questions is an important part of keeping happy, healthy and safe during puberty.**	**"Children are like caterpillars":** • like caterpillars, children don't look quite the same as when they are grown-ups; • as for the caterpillar in the story, the changes that happen to us may take us by surprise, but they are normal; • like caterpillars, children change to help them thrive in the wider world; • like caterpillars, growing children are very hungry – it takes a lot of energy to become a grown-up; • like caterpillars, growing children need safety and privacy while they develop.	Puberty Adolescence Teenager Hormones Emotional Physical Social Changes Privacy Boundaries Information Support Help

11) WET DREAMS – *Nocturnal emission*		
LEARNING THEMES	**THE METAPHOR AND HOW IT SUPPORTS LEARNING**	**KEY WORDS**

A normal part of puberty is when your body makes hormones that ready the sexual anatomy to reproduce when you're an adult – this includes wet dreams.
 	
In a male body, wet dreams are when sperm is released from the testicles, then fluids are added to make semen that leaves the penis through an erection and ejaculation.
 	
In a female body, the clitoris enlarges, and the vagina becomes lubricated.
 	
Wet dreams often occur at night during sleep.
 	
Wet dreams happen more often for some people than for others but are perfectly normal and nothing to be worried or ashamed about.
	"Having a wet dream is like a dragon discovering it can breathe fire":
	
	• just as dragons are supposed to breathe fire, wet dreams are natural;
	
	• like a dragon suddenly able to breathe fire, wet dreams are a sign that a human body can do new things;
	
	• this can take us by surprise, but it is a sign that the body is developing normally;
	
	• like a dragon newly able to breathe fire, wet dreams can bring good things but can also feel embarrassing to talk about.
		Puberty
		Hormones
		Reproduction
		Wet dreams
		Sexual anatomy
		Correct terminology:
		  Male: Penis, testicles, sperm, semen, erection, ejaculation
		  Female: Clitoris enlarges, vagina lubricates
		Normal
		Privacy
		Communication
		Support
		Help

12) PERIODS – *Menstruation*

LEARNING THEMES	THE METAPHOR AND HOW IT SUPPORTS LEARNING	KEY WORDS
Both females and males need to learn about the menstrual cycle to understand human reproduction. **Having knowledge about the menstrual cycle enables us to support those who have periods to manage the physical and emotional responses they experience.** **Females normally start their periods between the ages of 10 and 15 (it can start as early as 8 or as late as 17). Periods can be irregular to start with but, eventually, occur on average every 28 days.** **During the menstrual cycle, hormones release an egg from one ovary. The egg travels through the fallopian tube to the womb (uterus), where a lining of blood and fluids has developed to support a possible pregnancy.** **When the egg isn't fertilised by sperm (from a male), the lining is shed from the womb and passed through the vagina to the vulva as a period.** **A period lasts for approximately 3–5 days. Females manage their period by using pads, tampons or reusable products.**	**"A womb is like a hotel":** • like a hotel, a womb has extra comfy, plump red cushions and pillows; • like a hotel, a human reproductive system needs to be well maintained for its very important guest; • as in a hotel, a womb's soft furnishings are changed regularly; • as in a hotel, a human body has a system to pass messages around about "housekeeping" work; • as in a hotel, if a "guest" is inside the womb, its soft furnishings don't get changed.	Menstrual cycle Hormones Ovaries Eggs Fallopian tubes Womb/Uterus Embryo Lining shedding Menstruation/ Period Physical responses: cramps, sore breasts, bloating, cravings Emotional responses: pride, joy, irritability, mood swings Pads Tampons Period pants Cups Information Support Help

13) LOVE – *Romantic relationships*		
LEARNING THEMES	**THE METAPHOR AND HOW IT SUPPORTS LEARNING**	**KEY WORDS**
A normal and healthy part of growing up is to experience attraction and love for other people. **Having a crush or being in love can feel both great and confusing at the same time.** **Expressing your feelings about being attracted to or not attracted to someone can be difficult. You may be worried about being rejected or hurting someone's feelings.** **Having respect for other people's boundaries while understanding and expressing your own is a healthy and safe response.** **If you feel worried or confused about love and attraction, you should always talk to someone you trust.**	**"Love is like honey":** • like a bee and a flower, two beings can come together and make something special; • just as honey-making is a natural process, so is falling in love; • like honey-making, mutual love feels good – each supports the other – but sometimes, the match is not right, and people don't always have the same feelings for each other; • as for a bee and a flower, sometimes in love, your time together comes to an end, and that's ok.	Love Falling in love Having a crush Fancying someone Attraction Romance Mutual LGBT+ Different emotions Communication Falling out of love Rejection Respect Boundaries Consent Support Help

14) HOW A BABY IS MADE – *Reproduction*

LEARNING THEMES	THE METAPHOR AND HOW IT SUPPORTS LEARNING	KEY WORDS
Human reproduction is when a baby is made. The most common way for the egg and sperm to meet is when a female and a male have sex. The penis goes into the vagina, and semen (sperm and fluid) is released from the penis and travels through the vagina into the womb. If an egg has been recently released from an ovary, the sperm will meet it in the fallopian tube. This is called conception and starts the pregnancy. The baby will develop until it is ready to be born. If people cannot conceive a baby through sex, then there are other ways to help a sperm and egg meet. Babies need love, nurturing, safety and lots of care to thrive and grow. All babies are beautiful, no matter how they are made or how they come into a family.	"Babies are like sunflowers": • like sunflowers, to grow a baby, you need two things to come together; • like sunflowers, there are different ways to bring a baby into the world; • like sunflowers need sunshine, all babies need a loving environment to thrive; • like sunflowers, babies need a safe place to grow until they can make it on their own; • like sunflowers, each baby comes out looking different, but all are beautiful.	Human life cycle Menstrual cycle Reproduction Egg/Ovum Sperm Womb/Uterus Fallopian tube Penis Vagina Sex Pregnancy Fertility treatment Gestation Birth Babies Unique Family Love Nurture Safety Information

15) WHEN PEOPLE HAVE SEX – *Sexual activity*		
LEARNING THEMES	**THE METAPHOR AND HOW IT SUPPORTS LEARNING**	**KEY WORDS**
Sex is when people touch each other's private body parts, and it feels good. **People decide to have sex to share love and affection; some like to do it for fun, and sometimes it is also because they want to have a baby.** **People have to feel ready and be old enough and mature enough to have sex. In the UK you have to be 16 before you're legally able to make the decision to have sex. Lots of people wait till they are older than 16, and not everybody wants to have sex.** **In some cultures or religions, it is important to be married before you have sex.** **People should never be pressured into having sex or made to feel bad because they don't want to. Everybody gets to decide for themselves.**	**"Sex is like sharing a bike trip":** • like a bike trip, sex can be for the love of it, for fun and for a particular purpose; • like going on a bike trip, to have sex, you need to be responsible and feel ready – the circumstances and context also have to be right; • as with cycling, people need to be aware of the important equipment that makes sex feel good, fun and safe for everyone; • as on a bike trip, you can stop any time you want before or during sex.	Sex Private body parts Love and affection Mutual respect Boundaries Consent Maturity Readiness Choice Trust Responsibility Communication Safety Contraception Information Support Help

Section 4

The toolkits

1 Families
Families and people who care for me

R

Relationships education

LEARNING POINTS	KEYWORDS
Families provide security and stability. In a healthy family people show love, care and commitment. Families come in all shapes and sizes and may have different structures. Losing or gaining family members is a natural part of life. Each family have their own unique culture and background, and each should be respected. Families always change and can go through difficult times.	Love Care Security Stability Protection Responsibility Diverse Single parent Extended Grandparent Carer LGBT Adoption Fostering Young carers Marriage Stable relationship Separation Divorce Break-up Birth Death Support Help

DOI: 10.4324/9781003391654-4

FAMILIES

PART 1

Imagine there was a small seahorse in a big city aquarium, whose name was Squiggle. She lived with her four dads in a very comfortable corner tank. From where they were, they could just about see out of the aquarium window, and Squiggle was very proud of that window. She loved that out of all the sea creatures, they were the only family that could gaze upon the world beyond.

If Squiggle craned her long neck right around, she could see something especially strange out of that window. It was her favourite thing to stare at. It was almost as big as a house. It had a long brown cylinder with a fluffy green cloud on top. One long, boring evening when the aquarium was shut, she asked one of her seahorse dads what the thing was.

ASK THE CLASS: What does the dad seahorse say it is?

PART 2

Now imagine that the fluffy green cloud on the top of that object began to turn from green to all sorts of other colours – yellows, oranges, and finally browns. Eventually, pieces started to drop off it and fall to the ground.

The little seahorse shrieked so loudly that her friend Manny the octopus and all Manny's little brothers and sisters clung to their glass tanks in alarm. Squiggle went to her dads and she cried, "the tree is dying!"

The biggest of all her dads, a colourful seahorse she called Papa, gave her a nuzzle with his snout. He smiled and said not to worry.

ASK THE CLASS: What would Papa tell Squiggle about the tree?

FAMILIES

PART 3

One day, some men arrived at the aquarium and set up a green triangle with spikes all over it. It was decorated with coloured balls and lights. Because it was right in the middle of the aquarium, all the sea creatures could see it. "It's called a Christmas Tree," said Squiggle's friend Manny.

Squiggle howled with laughter: "that isn't a tree!" But Manny insisted. "Titan the Turtle told me, and he's 47 years old. He says they cut one down and bring it inside every year." Squiggle shook her head in disbelief.

ASK THE CLASS: Why didn't Squiggle believe Manny that it was a tree?

PART 4

Papa came over and interrupted gently. "Actually, Squiggle, trees come in all shapes and sizes. It's just like the families in this aquarium," he said, pointing toward Manny. "Your octopus friend over there has 322 siblings and you have none. Like the families here in the aquarium, every tree in the forest is different." Squiggle recovered her good temper and nodded, wisely. "I knew that, Papa," she said. "I know all about the world beyond. Or have you forgotten about my window?"

ASK THE CLASS: If the group of octopuses looks very different from the group of seahorses, does that mean one of them is not a family?

FAMILIES

The story has a message about families. Write what each part of the story might stand for.

This part of the story:

Is like:

DIFFERENT TYPES OF TREES   =   *Different types of family*

SQUIGGLE'S WINDOW   =   _____

_____

_____

SQUIGGLE'S BELIEF THAT THE   =   _____
CHRISTMAS TREE CAN'T BE A
TREE   _____

_____

WHEN A TREE'S LEAVES DROP   =   _____

_____

_____

A SEASON   =   _____

_____

_____

FAMILIES

This part of the story:		**Is like:**
DIFFERENT TYPES OF TREES	=	*Different types of family*
SQUIGGLE'S WINDOW	=	*The small window of experience each of us has of the world*
SQUIGGLE'S BELIEF THAT THE CHRISTMAS TREE CAN'T BE A TREE	=	*People thinking there's only one kind of family*
WHEN A TREE'S LEAVES DROP	=	*A family bereavement*
A SEASON	=	*A generation*

LEARNING POINT

WHAT CAN WE SAY ABOUT FAMILIES?

- Families are like trees because they, too, come in all different shapes and sizes.
- Families are like trees because people come and go, like leaves.

The toolkits

How are trees like families? Match up the story cards (1–5) with the explanation cards (A–E).

STORY CARDS

EXPLANATION CARDS

	STORY CARDS		EXPLANATION CARDS
1	Trees come in ALL DIFFERENT SHAPES AND SIZES.	A	Our families are usually the people we trust most in the whole world. They can give us protection and shelter, like standing under a big chestnut tree in a rainstorm. That can make it easy to take them for granted, but just like other relationships, our families need to feel love and appreciation.
2	Trees can be BIG OR SMALL.	B	There are times when a tree grows beautiful flowers or delicious fruit. But there are other times when its leaves fall. Just like this, a family may go through good times and hard times. Families change, shrink and grow. By standing firm and supporting each other, families can get through challenges.
3	Trees can PROVIDE SHELTER but NEED NOURISHMENT.	C	A tree needs its roots to suck water and nutrients from the soil. It needs its branches to grow tall and find the light. And it needs its leaves to soak up the sun. Just like that, even the youngest family members have responsibilities – whether that's keeping the house tidy or being quiet in the morning.
4	EACH PART of a tree has A JOB TO DO.	D	A family can have just two people in it and be small, like a bonsai tree. Or families can be like a giant oak, with hundreds of branches. The phrase "nuclear family" means one household with one or more adults and their child or children. An "extended family" may include grandparents, cousins and more.
5	Trees can LOSE PARTS as well as GROWING NEW ONES.	E	Families can look as different as a pine tree and a holly bush. They can have one dad, two mums, a foster parent or a grandparent in charge. There are about 73,000 species of tree in the world. How many different kinds of families can you think of?

1 matches with ___   3 matches with ___   5 matches with ___

2 matches with ___   4 matches with ___

FAMILIES

EXTENSION ACTIVITIES

 Ask students, "If your family were a tree, what kind of tree would it be?" Ask them to draw, paint or collage the tree that best represents their family.

 Get the students to choose a famous fictional family (for example, the Incredibles, the Borrowers, or the family in Roald Dahl's *The Witches*). How is that family different from their family? What would they like and not like about being in that family? If these examples are so different, what makes each of them a family?

 Ask students to take a page of lined paper and fold it in two. In one section, write about a time when a family might "blossom." In the other, write about a time when a family might "shed its leaves."

ANSWERS for the card matching activity

1 matches with E
2 matches with D
3 matches with A
4 matches with C
5 matches with B

TEACHING NOTES

- **Diversity:** Become familiar with the diverse cultural backgrounds represented within the classroom. Are any protected characteristics represented in the group of learners or in their family? Do all the children feel visible and represented in a positive and inclusive way during the session?
- **Children's home circumstances:** For break-ups, divorce or children in care or on the edge of care it can be helpful to use the metaphor to emphasise that roots can recover after disruption and may be invisible but always under the soil. Signpost to sources that can support and help.
- **Family ill health or grief:** Be mindful of any child who is worried about a family member or has experienced grief. The tree metaphor may help children whose families are going through difficult circumstances to think about the seasonal and cyclical way in which trees blossom, fruit and shed leaves.

2 Friendships
Healthy friendships

R
Relationships education

LEARNING POINTS	KEYWORDS
Healthy friendships make us feel happy and secure. Friendships need to be nurtured with respect, honesty, care and loyalty. Friendships can change with time and can have ups and downs. Good friends show each other respect and honesty even when they disagree or have a fall-out. When people experience unhealthy friendships, they can get support from people they trust to stand up for themselves and change the relationship.	Respect Truthfulness Care Trust Loyalty Kindness Generosity Inclusive Conflict Fall-out Communication Mental well-being Support Help

DOI: 10.4324/9781003391654-5

FRIENDSHIPS

Read this story aloud to the group, using the prompt questions to encourage active listening.

PART 1

Imagine a classmate called Lal. You like Lal. They have a bit of an air of mystery about them; plus, they're a touch quieter than the other kids and not so rough. You're Lal's desk partner this year and, ever since the start of the Autumn term, you notice there's always a book on Lal's desk. It's called *The Dragon God*; it has a fiery orange, glittery cover with a beautiful dragon on the front. One day you ask Lal about it, and the words come flooding out. Lal says it glows with magic; it makes them laugh out loud; the exciting bits make their stomach churn. Every time they open it, Lal explains with bright eyes, the world around them melts away.

ASK THE CLASS: What books have you loved like that?

PART 2

Lal never wants to read anything else, and they carry the book with them wherever they go. A few weeks into term, you notice them beginning to change. Purple is no longer their favourite colour – everything they wear seems to be orange, like the book. They've started sitting out of football at lunchtime to re-read certain chapters. When you come to get them, they shake their head – but you don't understand the word they used. Apparently, it's how people talk in the book: in a special, secret language. Eventually, you give up and go away.

ASK THE CLASS: Does Lal have a healthy relationship with that book?

FRIENDSHIPS

Read this story aloud to the group, using the prompt questions to encourage active listening.

PART 3

Things go from bad to worse. One day, you see Lal take *The Dragon God* carefully out from inside a plastic sleeve that was inside a shoebox that they carried inside their bag. You make a grab for the book, joking, "it's not the crown jewels!" and the corner of the cover creases and tears slightly.

Lal's face goes hard with fury. They shove your hand away, drawing blood as their fingernail accidentally scrapes down the skin of your hand.

ASK THE CLASS: If a book gets bent or torn, can it be repaired? Will it be any less wonderful?

PART 4

The next day, Lal apologises. Holding out the book, they say, "For you to borrow," and then swallow hard. Lal's face is pale but determined. You have an idea. "Let's walk up to the charity bookshop," you say. "We can see if they've got any of the *Goosebumps* series – they're really good."

As it turns out, *Goosebumps* was too scary for Lal, but you swap it for one of the new fantasy series you're into. Before long, you and Lal are regulars at the bookshop. By summer, other colours have crept back into Lal's life – blue and white and even purple – to join those worn old orange hoodies. In both of your bedrooms, yours and Lal's, the bookshelves are a rainbow of fun and adventure.

ASK THE CLASS: Does having a full bookshelf mean Lal loves *The Dragon God* any less?

FRIENDSHIPS

The story has a message about friendships. Write what each part of the story might stand for.

This part of the story:

Is like:

THE FEELINGS A FAVOURITE BOOK CAN BRING   =   *The feelings a close friendship can bring*

LAL'S UNHEALTHY OBSESSION WITH THEIR FAVOURITE BOOK   =   _____
_____
_____
_____

A TEAR IN A BOOK   =   _____
_____
_____
_____

REPAIRING A BOOK   =   _____
_____
_____
_____

A FULL, COLOURFUL BOOKSHELF   =   _____
_____
_____
_____

FRIENDSHIPS

This part of the story:		Is like:
THE FEELINGS A FAVOURITE BOOK CAN BRING	=	*The feelings a close friendship can bring*
LAL'S UNHEALTHY OBSESSION WITH THEIR FAVOURITE BOOK	=	*An unhealthy relationship with a friend*
A TEAR IN A BOOK	=	*An argument with a friend*
REPAIRING A BOOK	=	*Making up after an argument*
A FULL, COLOURFUL BOOKSHELF	=	*A life full of different and diverse friendships*

LEARNING POINT

WHAT CAN WE SAY ABOUT FRIENDSHIPS?

- A good friendship is like a good book because it can bring comfort and joy and can survive a bit of wear and tear.
- Sharing a book doesn't make it any less good and neither does sharing a friendship.

How are books like friendships? Match up the story cards (1–5) with the explanation cards (A–E).

STORY CARDS

EXPLANATION CARDS

1	**Books can MAKE YOU FEEL HAPPY AND SECURE even if you are facing challenges in life.**	A	If a book gets a bit of a tear, it can usually be repaired, and it's no less enjoyable. It's the same with friendships. Even best friends come into conflict sometimes, but that doesn't have to mean they're ruined forever. It's how you patch it up again afterward that counts.
2	**You need to treat books nicely, but they CAN SURVIVE SOME WEAR AND TEAR.**	B	You can still love a book if you haven't read it for years. And friendships don't expire either. You don't have to see your friends all the time to call them friends. Good friends will stay loyal to each other through thick and thin, even if time and distance get in the way.
3	**You DON'T NEED TO STICK TO JUST ONE FAVOURITE book.**	C	Sometimes you'll start a book that you don't get along with – it's a struggle to keep going. In the same way, not everybody gets along with their friends all the time, and that's ok. Some friendships can get too challenging or even unhealthy. It's ok to take a break, reset the relationship, and even pause for a while.
4	**YOU CAN TAKE A BREAK AND COME BACK to a book.**	D	A wonderful book can help us escape our real-world concerns or even show us how to deal with our problems. That's also the sort of comfort and joy we can get from being with friends. They can take the weight off our shoulders in hard times.
5	**If you try a book that doesn't suit you, IT'S OK TO STOP.**	E	You wouldn't want to read just one book for the rest of your life. In the same way, we don't need to stick to just one friend at a time. Like books, we get something different and unique from each of our friends. Having several doesn't make each one any less valuable.

1 matches with ___   3 matches with ___   5 matches with ___

2 matches with ___   4 matches with ___

FRIENDSHIPS

EXTENSION ACTIVITIES

Choose a friend or family member who you love. Imagine they are the hero of a good book. Draw a book cover for it and give it a title (that doesn't include their name).

Play a quick-fire game. Get into pairs and list as many fictional "best friendships" as you can in 60 seconds, taking the school or library bookshelf as inspiration. Pick one and find the passage in the book that best illustrates that friendship.

Divide a page in half and write down some "things a good friend does" (for example, "sticks up for you in front of other people"). For each one, see if you can think of a counter example – something you might find in an unhealthy friendship. Share your page with others and see if you have similar or different lists.

ANSWERS for the card matching activity

1 matches with D

2 matches with A

3 matches with E

4 matches with B

5 matches with C

TEACHING NOTES

- **Classroom conflict:** Be mindful of individuals or friendship groups experiencing unhealthy friendships or conflict. Can you use the activity to address any current friendship issues?
- **Group management:** Carefully manage how groups of learners are formed for the activities to address any issues or concerns.

3 Respecting difference
Diversity

R
Relationships education

LEARNING POINTS	KEYWORDS
There are lots of similarities and differences between people: how they look; their character, personality, preferences, culture and background. Other people may be different but showing respect and treating them as equals will make us learn and appreciate new things. We often have more in common than meets the eye. When we communicate well and show interest, we can focus on similarities rather than differences.	Similar Different Equal Stereotype Respect Diversity Attitude Curiosity Courtesy Manners Choices Preferences Beliefs Culture LGBT Gender Ability Age Race/Ethnicity Discrimination Prejudice Racism Bullying Support Help

DOI: 10.4324/9781003391654-6

RESPECTING DIFFERENCE

Read this story aloud to the group, using the prompt questions to encourage active listening.

PART 1

Imagine that it's 2093 and World War IV is raging. People in your country have had to flee their homes. You and your family move to Iceland (where the weather is now warmer and sunnier than it is at home). A nice, elderly couple called Mr and Mrs Petersen take you in.

You and your parents have had enough food in your packs to keep you going for a while, but tonight you sit down at the Petersens' dinner table for the first time. Proudly, they bring a dish to the table that they call Swaasat: it looks just like the inside of a pie, but it smells a little bit like rotting fish. The Petersons tell you it's made of seal meat.

ASK THE CLASS: How would you feel about being served Swaasat?

PART 2

That's where things start to go wrong. First your dad won't thank the Icelandic Spirits, which is a custom that most locals honour at mealtimes. The Spirits are kind of like ghosts, and Mr Peterson says that you can talk to them by whistling. "I've never talked to something I can't see," your dad says, "let alone whistled at it."

Then your dad turns to examine the seal stew and point-blank refuses to eat it. At home, he would only eat curry, burgers, and fish and chips on a Friday. To be honest, he prefers a battered sausage, but if there's someone to impress, he'll stretch to a piece of cod.

"That's disgusting," he mutters under his breath. "It's just ... unnatural."

ASK THE CLASS: Do you agree with dad?

Read this story aloud to the group, using the prompt questions to encourage active listening.

PART 3

Now, in this new world, people who speak different languages can understand each other because of a new invention called ComPods. They work by each person sticking a blob, like chewing gum, behind their ear lobes, and then whatever's said comes to their brain directly in their chosen language.

Tonight, the night of your first dinner in Iceland, the Petersons must have their ComPods turned up too high. When dad says what he says, even though he practically whispers it, Mr Peterson puts down his fork and turns his wrinkled face toward dad with a sly look in his eyes.

ASK THE CLASS: When two people are from different places, what do they need to understand each other properly?

PART 4

Mr Peterson says in a calm, quiet voice: "I went to England, as a boy, and tried some of what you call cheese and crackers. That cheese!" Mr Peterson screws up his face, wafts his hands in front of his mouth and says, "It was so sour it made my tongue tingle in pain."

You think about cheese sandwiches, and your stomach grumbles. Mr Peterson carries on: "You don't have to enjoy Swaasat, but I will ask you not to criticise it."

Dad unfolds his arms and has a think. "That's fair cop. And in return, I'll be getting in some chips on a Friday, my friend," says Dad. "Now, chips...," Mr Peterson grins. "That's what I lived on in England. The only food I could stand."

ASK THE CLASS: What's weirder, cheddar cheese or seal stew?

RESPECTING DIFFERENCE

The story has a message about diversity and respect. Write what each part of the story might stand for.

This part of the story:

Is like:

AN UNFAMILIAR DISH = *People from other cultures*

FAMILIAR FOOD LIKE BURGERS AND FISH AND CHIPS = _____
_____
_____

DAD'S RUDENESS ABOUT THE STEW = _____
_____
_____

SPEAKING DIFFERENT LANGUAGES = _____
_____
_____

COMPODS, THE NEW TRANSLATION INVENTION = _____
_____
_____

RESPECTING DIFFERENCE

This part of the story:		Is like:
AN UNFAMILIAR DISH	=	*People from other cultures*
FAMILIAR FOOD LIKE BURGERS AND FISH & CHIPS	=	*Cultures you are familiar and comfortable with*
DAD'S RUDENESS ABOUT THE STEW	=	*Prejudice or racism about people from different cultures*
SPEAKING DIFFERENT LANGUAGES	=	*Misunderstanding between cultures*
COMPODS, THE NEW TRANSLATION INVENTION	=	*Finding things in common with people who are different from you*

LEARNING POINT

WHAT CAN WE SAY ABOUT RESPECT?
- Respect is like a new food because even though unfamiliar things can feel scary, it's worth giving them a chance.

How are new foods like different people? Match up the story cards (1–5) with the explanation cards (A–E).

STORY CARDS

EXPLANATION CARDS

	Story Cards		Explanation Cards
1	**EACH OF US HAS ONLY TRIED A TINY SLICE of the food the world has to offer.**	A	Things you've never tried before can seem weird or even wrong or bad. That goes for new foods but also other people. It's easy to decide something is bad without trying to see it from a different point of view.
2	**If a food is NEW to you, that DOESN'T MEAN IT'S BAD.**	B	There are so many different foods and dishes from all over the world. There are also thousands of different ways to be. No two people look, speak and behave exactly the same – or believe the same things.
3	**Trying new foods can make people feel NERVOUS.**	C	Whether it's food or something different, try to feel interested and curious when you come across something new. Why waste life feeling suspicious?
4	**An ADVENTUROUS ATTITUDE to food will help you make the most of things.**	D	It won't hurt anyone if you chew with your mouth open, but table manners can help you to feel confident. It's the same when you're faced with a new situation: being polite can send out the right messages about you.
5	**When it comes to food, MANNERS MATTER.**	E	Experiencing new things can make you feel nervous, frightened, even disgusted but also excited or proud. It's the same for food and other things about people's cultures. Stepping outside of your comfort zone takes practice.

1 matches with ___   3 matches with ___   5 matches with ___

2 matches with ___   4 matches with ___

RESPECTING DIFFERENCE

EXTENSION ACTIVITIES

Have "speed conversations" for 30 seconds each with several classmates. Try to find out one thing that is similar and one thing that is different about your family backgrounds (this could be about your traditions, your beliefs or the food you eat).

Individually, write a few sentences to describe a fictional world that is completely different from our own. Include some customs, manners and habits that we would all find very strange. Now get into pairs and share your worlds with each other. Talk about what a stranger from these worlds would think of our own cultures.

Research a chosen culture that is different from your own on the internet or in the library. Write a list of values, beliefs and customs commonly shared in that culture. Select one value, belief or custom that you would like to "test out" in your own life – for example, "Zakat" in Islam, which means "charitable giving."

ANSWERS for the card matching activity

1 matches with B
2 matches with A
3 matches with E
4 matches with C
5 matches with D

TEACHING NOTES

- **Diversity:** Become familiar with the diverse cultural backgrounds represented within the classroom. Are any protected characteristics represented in the group of learners or in their communities? Do all the children feel visible and represented in a positive and inclusive way during the session? Can you use the toolkit to address any issues experienced within the group of learners?
- **Policies:** Check your setting's anti-bullying, behaviour and equality policies.

4 Making friends online
Digital relationships

R Relationships education

LEARNING POINTS	KEYWORDS
Making friends online can be fun and a good opportunity to learn about new things. There are risks to making friends online when you don't know them in real life: they include meeting people who want to take advantage of you, harm you, or steal your personal information. There are tools, techniques and software that can help keep children safe when interacting with others online. Online safety also includes recognising when a friendship is healthy and being critical of shared information. Just like with face-to-face friendships, it's important to know where to go for help and support.	Online behaviour Devices Social media Positive/Negative Connecting Accepting (a request) Sharing Friends Strangers Personal Privacy Information Face-to-face Anonymous Safety Risk Harassment Bullying Trolling Mental health Physical health Report Support Help

DOI: 10.4324/9781003391654-7

Read this story aloud to the group, using the prompt questions to encourage active listening.

PART 1

Rock Face climbing club is in an old church. It smells chalky and a bit sweaty, but it's Ashley's favourite place in the world. He goes there three times a week with his friends Mark and Ellen to race them up the walls. Today, though, the three friends walk in pulling their "worst day in the world" faces at each other. It's Half Term club, meaning it's the week when you're forced to queue up behind clueless beginners from two years below you in school and do bouldering, all day, every day. Bouldering means messing about on the low walls, never going more than a few feet up. The three friends put their heads together and begin to whisper.

ASK THE CLASS: Who thinks climbing sounds fun? Who thinks it sounds dangerous? Can something be both?

PART 2

The plan is this: Ashley, Mark and Ellen will sneak off during the safety lecture. Their absence will hardly be noticed, what with 35 newbies milling around. They'll head around the back of the club to the Wall of Doom. That's the hardest wall in the club: it goes all the way up inside what used to be the church spire, and it has the tiniest handholds you've ever seen. Best of all, it's completely hidden from where the teachers are all still kitting up the little ones.

Ellen's the best, so she's up first, with Ashley underneath on the ropes. She makes a strong start, reaching what would usually be their top height in under two minutes. "You're going great," Ashley whispers as loudly as he dares from underneath her, and Ellen gives a happy tug on the rope. That's when Ashley gives a little frown and looks at his hands. His blood runs cold.

ASK THE CLASS: What do you think has happened?

MAKING FRIENDS ONLINE

PART 3

Ashley feels suddenly sick. He hadn't felt Ellen's tug on the safety ropes he's holding – not even the slightest twitch. He looks to the floor in panic. The rope is looped twice and pulled tight, just like it should be, but he hasn't passed it through the metal D-ring (the most important part). Ellen, who has just begun to tackle the wall's notorious overhang, is attached to nothing.

High up above, she gives a grunt of frustration at a handhold just out of reach. Ashley should tell someone, but... "You're really high," he stutters, not wanting to freak her out. "Come down a bit?" Ellen laughs and says, "Chill!" And that's when it happens. Her arm flails. A foot slips. Ashley always tries to pause the video in his mind at this point. But it won't stop.

ASK THE CLASS: Why do you think Ashley didn't tell someone?

PART 4

Everything's a blur. Someone cries out; Ashley doesn't realise it's him. There are staff running. The ambulance. The hospital waiting room. Ellen's parents, talking in low voices to the doctor.

Alone in his room, Ashley closes his eyes and tries to shake the thoughts out of his head. He's lying on his bed, where he's been for most of the summer, hiding and listening to music.

Ellen had broken two leg bones, and it took her two months to get completely better. But now she's here at the front door, ready to walk round the corner and back to the Rock Face club. Ashley can hear his dad letting her down gently, "he's not ready, Ellen love." Ellen might be back to normal, but he's not sure he ever will be.

ASK THE CLASS: How were Ellen and Ashley each affected by the accident?

MAKING FRIENDS ONLINE

The story has a message about making friends online. Write what each part of the story might stand for.

This part of the story:		Is like:

GOING ROCK CLIMBING   =   *Making friends online*

ROPES AND HARNESS   =   _____
                                _____
                                _____

GOING UP HIGH   =   _____
                                _____
                                _____

CLIMBING INSTRUCTORS   =   _____
                                _____
                                _____

A CLIMBING ACCIDENT   =   _____
                                _____
                                _____

MAKING FRIENDS ONLINE

This part of the story:		**Is like:**
GOING ROCK CLIMBING	=	*Making friends online*
ROPES AND HARNESS	=	*The technology that is used to keep children safe online*
GOING UP HIGH	=	*Doing something online that has risks*
CLIMBING INSTRUCTORS	=	*The adults e.g., our parents who can help us if things go wrong*
A CLIMBING ACCIDENT	=	*Coming to harm through the internet*

LEARNING POINT

WHAT CAN WE SAY ABOUT MAKING FRIENDS ONLINE?
- Online friendships are like rock climbing because they come with risks, but there are ways to stay safe.

How are online friendships like rock climbing? Match up the story cards (1–5) with the explanation cards (A–E).

STORY CARDS **EXPLANATION CARDS**

	STORY CARDS		EXPLANATION CARDS
1	Rock climbing CAN BE FUN.	A	There's a great view from the top of a rock face. Going online also gives us a chance to understand life from a different point of view. We can see things and talk to people from all around the world.
2	Rock climbing CAN EXPAND YOUR HORIZONS.	B	You wouldn't start a climb without an adult at the bottom to keep you safe. In the same way, if you're talking to friends online, an adult needs to know that you're doing it. Knowing that someone you trust is keeping an eye on your safety leaves you free to have fun without worrying.
3	There's a RISK OF GETTING HURT when rock climbing.	C	Hobbies are for enjoyment. They usually give people the chance to meet similar people and make friends. It's no different online; the apps we use often come with the opportunity to chat to others. It can be fun to talk about things you care about with people who feel the same way.
4	You NEED SAFETY EQUIPMENT AND TRAINING for rock climbing.	D	You wouldn't dream of going up a rock face without ropes and harnesses or without knowing how to use them. That's how we need to treat online apps or websites in which we talk to other people. Adults can help you make sure any online devices you use are set up properly to keep you safe.
5	SOMEONE TRUSTWORTHY NEEDS TO BE READY TO HELP when you go rock climbing.	E	Some fun things come with risks – rock climbing is one, and using the internet is another. Things can go wrong that aren't necessarily your fault, and people can get hurt. We need to tread carefully and think before we take our next steps.

1 matches with ___ 3 matches with ___ 5 matches with ___
2 matches with ___ 4 matches with ___

MAKING FRIENDS ONLINE

EXTENSION ACTIVITIES

Use Google's "Interland" game to explore four areas of internet safety: the "Mindful Mountain" (share with care), "Tower of Treasure" (secure your secrets), "Kind Kingdom" (it's cool to be kind) or "Reality River" (don't fall for fake).
Share your findings with others.
This game can be accessed here: https://beinternetawesome .withgoogle.com/

Make a persuasive poster that tells people what you need to stay safe online. Draw the following climbing tools: harness, partner and handholds. Write a label to say what the equivalent tool is for online safety.

Watch the SMART crew videos from Childnet.
The videos can be accessed here: https://www.childnet.com/ resources/the-adventures-of-kara-winston-and-the-smart-crew/.
Share one thing you want to think about when you use the internet in future.

ANSWERS for the card matching activity

1 matches with C

2 matches with A

3 matches with E

4 matches with D

5 matches with B

TEACHING NOTES

- **Popular media sites:** Familiarise yourself with the popular internet/social media sites used by children in the class. These change with time.

- **Incidences of issues or concerns:** Has any inappropriate online activity (online bullying, trolling, harassment, inappropriate sharing) created issues or concerns within the class? Can you use the toolkit to address these issues?

- **Safeguarding:** Follow your setting's Child Protection and Safeguarding policies and speak with the Designated Safeguarding Lead regarding **any** concerns about a child's welfare: disclosure or indicators of abuse, neglect or exploitation. Signpost to sources of support and help.

5 What you find online
Appropriate online content

R Relationships education

LEARNING POINTS	KEYWORDS
The internet is a great source of information and entertainment. It is very popular; some use it more than others.	Appropriate / inappropriate
	Harmful content
	Safety
	Risk
Knowing how to manage time online is part of mental health and wellbeing.	Age restrictions
	Curiosity
	Pressure
Some online platforms and sites come with age restrictions to keep people safe from inappropriate content.	Sexualised imagery / Pornography
	Mental health
	Block
Exposure to inappropriate content can be a result of being curious, unaware or pressure from another person and is not always deliberate.	Report
	Support
	Help
It is important to know how to deal with inappropriate content such as blocking, reporting and finding support and help to talk things through.	

DOI: 10.4324/9781003391654-8

WHAT YOU FIND ONLINE

Read this story aloud to the group, using the prompt questions to encourage active listening.

PART 1

Imagine a kitchen boy called Elias, who lived hundreds of years ago in the time of castles and servants and when simple food was cooked over open fires. One day, the local sorcerer gives Elias the gift of time travel: he can spend one hour in the future. Elias picks, at random, a year in the 2020s. He begins to whirl through time. The mud and wood of the medieval kitchen blur around him and become smooth, pink walls, and a plush bed.

Elias finds himself standing in what must be some sort of princess's bedroom. He can tell, because the place is sparkling clean and there are beautiful, pointless things everywhere. Hanging on the door is a soft, purple gown with pink shapes woven onto it, and – look! – there on the table – a whole shiny, crinkling bag full of jewels!

ASK THE CLASS: What kind of room has Elias stepped into in the future?

PART 2

Elias inspects the crinkly bag, which is labelled "Fun Pack." *Fun!* he thinks – *like hopscotch or nine-pins*). It contains little rocks that look like jewels, but they are spongy and coated in... yes! Those crystals must be sugar. The only person Elias knows who has ever tasted sugar is the lord of the manor back home.

In five seconds flat, Elias has eaten every jewel in the bag, eyes wide with pleasure. In the next room, he finds and gobbles up a box full of delicious-smelling brown sticks. They're filled with something that looks like mud, but he has never tasted anything so good and so sweet. He finds a second box, and begins to tuck in.

Elias only stops when he feels a rumbling in his tummy. Something so wonderful can't be poisonous, can it? Elias gives a soft moan. He picks up a large squashy boot lined with sheep's wool and is violently sick inside it.

ASK THE CLASS: What has Elias found in this modern house?

Read this story aloud to the group, using the prompt questions to encourage active listening.

PART 3

At that moment, a girl walks in through the white door. The princess herself! "Your majesty!" Elias scrambles to his feet and into a deep bow. Before the princess can scream, he garbles the whole story and begs the gracious royal lady for her help. He then crumples back down to his knees and clutches his stomach again. As his head comes to rest on a shelf, Elias glimpses another box – this one labelled Whiskey Truffles. "Ah, my lady!" he cries. "Some more sugar will restore my health and strength!"

ASK THE CLASS: What doesn't Elias know about sweets? And sweets with alcohol in them?

PART 4

"No!" the princess shrieks. "Mum and Dad will kill me!"

"My lady," gasps Elias. "I will protect you."

She laughs. "No, I just mean, that I'm not allowed those." The royal girl kneels beside him and gives him a compassionate pat. "Look, all those fruit gums you ate – it takes me a month to get through a bag like that. They're not poisonous but, well, they sort of are if you eat too many."

She runs out and comes back holding a box of colourful jewels, just like the ones Elias had first enjoyed. "If my watch is right, you've got about five minutes left here. Take these with you, but just one per day, ok?"

ASK THE CLASS: If you could have all the chocolate and sweets you wanted, how much would you eat?

WHAT YOU FIND ONLINE

The story has a message about what you find online. Write what each part of the story might stand for.

This part of the story: **Is like:**

SWEET TREATS   =   *Fun apps or websites*

A PORTION OR PACKET OF
SWEETS   =   _____
                                       _____
                                       _____

CHOCOLATES WITH ALCOHOL   =   _____
                                       _____
                                       _____

FEELING SICK FROM EATING
UNHEALTHY FOOD   =   _____
                                       _____

READING THE NUTRITION
INFORMATION ON A PACKET OF   =   _____
SWEETS   _____
                                       _____

WHAT YOU FIND ONLINE

This part of the story:		Is like:
SWEET TREATS	=	*Fun apps or websites*
A PORTION OR PACKET OF SWEETS	=	*The right, safe amount of online activity*
CHOCOLATES WITH ALCOHOL	=	*Websites meant only for adults*
FEELING SICK FROM EATING UNHEALTHY FOOD	=	*A "gross" or uncomfortable feeling when you come across something you shouldn't online*
READING THE NUTRITION INFORMATION ON A PACKET OF SWEETS	=	*Getting help from adults about what's appropriate for children online*

LEARNING POINT

WHAT CAN WE SAY ABOUT THE INTERNET?
- The internet is like sugary food because it's bad for you to have too much (or the wrong kind), so we need to set limits.

67

How are sweet treats like what you find online? Match up the story cards (1–5) with the explanation cards (A–E).

STORY CARDS

EXPLANATION CARDS

	STORY CARDS		EXPLANATION CARDS
1	Sweet treats are everywhere! They're POPULAR WITH KIDS.	A	Most children understand that grown-ups have to stop them from eating too much sugar. It's not to spoil their fun but to keep them safe. Like sweet treats, there's a lot that's great about the internet, but adults have to help children protect themselves from some of its risky sides, too.
2	You can't always trust your senses to tell you when you've HAD TOO MUCH of a sweet treat.	B	Some of what's on the internet is only meant for adults and not children, but, like sweet treats, this content doesn't always come with a health warning. The people making money from selling unsafe or unhealthy things aren't always trying as hard as they could to keep children safe from them.
3	Sweet treats DON'T ALWAYS COME WITH A WARNING if they are bad for CHILDREN.	C	If you do come across something on the internet that's meant for adults, that can feel wrong or bad – a sort of "gross" feeling. We can compare that to eating too many treats or eating sweets only made for adults (for example, ones that contain alcohol). It would be important to ask a grown-up for help if that happened.
4	Some sweet treats can MAKE YOU FEEL BAD OR WRONG.	D	Sugar tastes good to most people, but if they followed their senses and ate as much as they wanted, it could harm their health. It's the same with the internet: if an app, game or site is fun, it can be hard to stop, but we need a "varied diet" of different activities.
5	GROWN-UPS CAN HELP SET LIMITS on sweet treats and support you when you're not sure.	E	Sweets are cheap and easy to get hold of in shops, playgrounds and homes. Kids love them, and the temptation is everywhere. It can feel the same with the internet. When a game, app or website is popular, it might feel like everyone is on it all the time.

1 matches with ___   3 matches with ___   5 matches with ___
2 matches with ___   4 matches with ___

WHAT YOU FIND ONLINE

EXTENSION ACTIVITIES

Write your own story about someone travelling through time to the present day (from either the past or the future). Include one thing they find wonderful, one thing they find disgusting and one danger they encounter.

Test yourself:

- If a person spends 2 hours per day online, how many whole days is that every year?
- What adds up to more screen time: 1.5 hours per day or 9 hours per week?
- They say it takes 10,000 hours of practice to become an expert in anything. How many hours per day would this be if you want to be an expert by the time you're 18?

Make some "top trumps" cards (using a blank template from the internet) for apps, online games or websites that you know about. Give each one a score out of ten for fun-ometer, safety, popularity and learning.

ANSWERS for the card matching activity

1 matches with E

2 matches with D

3 matches with B

4 matches with C

5 matches with A

TEACHING NOTES

- **Classroom issues:** Has any inappropriate online activity (such as sharing of inappropriate content) created issues or concerns within the class? Can you use the toolkit to address these issues?
- **Safeguarding:** Follow your setting's Child Protection and Safeguarding policies and speak with the Designated Safeguarding Lead regarding **any** concerns about a child's welfare: disclosure or indicators of abuse, neglect or exploitation. Signpost to sources of support and help.
- **Sexualised imagery/pornography:** Children are often, inadvertently, exposed to sexualised imagery out of curiosity or through pressure. This may become apparent during the session. Do not reprimand the children but, if appropriate, reiterate that:
  - this content is meant for adults, not children,
  - it likely does not represent real-life relationships and sex between people who care for each other,
  - they can speak to a trusted adult if they are worried and can get help to check safety features and filters on devices and platforms.

6 Respecting all genders
Gender equality

R
Relationships
education

LEARNING POINTS	KEYWORDS
Gender equality means that everyone has the same rights and opportunities. People have the right to feel safe and be treated with respect and equality – no matter their sex or gender. We may look and feel different from others but if you look closely and communicate respectfully then you'll see that people have more similarities than differences. Sexism is prejudice or discrimination based on sex or gender. We have laws and rules to protect against gender-based discrimination, bullying, harassment, abuse and violence. Bystander intervention is when each of us can challenge and/or report any disrespect when we see it.	Gender Expectations Stereotypes Equality Similarity Difference LGBT Choices Beliefs Culture Healthy relationships Respectful Communication Power Oppression Discrimination Sexism Bullying Harassment Abuse Violence Report Support Help

DOI: 10.4324/9781003391654-9

Read this story aloud to the group, using the prompt questions to encourage active listening.

RESPECTING ALL GENDERS

PART 1

On the planet Mathematica, most of the population is either a Percentage (known as a Percie) or a Fraction (known as a Frazzle). The Percies and the Frazzles must get along and work together, for there is much work to be done on Mathematica. The notebooks in which they are scribbled sometimes flap and tear in the planet's stormy winds of ignorance, so they must continuously be pinned down with tent pegs made of "hard reason." The Frazzles hold them down and the Percies hammer them in.

You would think that all this teamwork would have made firm friends of the numbers of Mathematica. You would think that harmony reigned, and when the pages of the notebooks closed for the night after a hard day's hammering, that here was a society of equals. And it was, until one day, the Frazzles discovered a dangerous substance called rubber.

ASK THE CLASS: What do you think happens when the Frazzles discover rubber?

PART 2

Armed with fearful weapons they called rubbers, some Frazzles began to abuse their power. They spread out over the pages, talking loudly. When a particularly arrogant fraction called Half was around, Fifty Percent kept its head down and tried hard to fit within the lines. The merciless gang of thirds was even worse: they tormented a Percie called Thirty Three percent, who had a particularly long tail, until it began to keep itself wrapped up in shame. Did that stop the gang of Frazzles? On the contrary: one day, they did the unthinkable. They took Thirty Three's percentage sign and rubbed it clean off the page. Robbed of its sign, the percentage promptly blew up like a balloon. It took four days to deflate the poor number all the way back down to size.

ASK THE CLASS: How did one group begin to dominate the others?

RESPECTING ALL GENDERS

Read this story aloud to the group, using the prompt questions to encourage active listening.

PART 3

The joke caught on: it became quite commonplace to wipe out a Percie's percent sign. Each time, the Frazzles laughed like windbags; they couldn't – or, perhaps, they didn't want to – see the look of pain on the Percies' digits. Sometimes the Percies would laugh along because, well, what else can you do?

Percentages around Mathematica began to pack up and leave. So, in sympathy, did a small, studious group of numbers called the Decimals. As the numbers became imbalanced, the notebooks in which they all lived begin to tilt to the side, their pages flapping harder than ever. Mathematica had become a dangerously unequal place; so much so, that it threatened to spin quite off its axis.

ASK THE CLASS: What can you do about silly but hurtful jokes?

PART 4

One day, the Frazzles had the shock of their lives to see the Percies marching back over the horizon. You see, they and the Decimals hadn't left for good. They had gone to request an audience with their leader, the Great Infinity. Curved and elegant, the Great Infinity was actually leading the procession home. It stopped to read a proclamation: "Percentages, Fractions and Decimals are different but equal," declared the Great Infinity. "None shall oppress the other." To this day, that moment is still remembered on Mathematica as National Equality Day, when equal signs are hung all over the planet in the Percies' honour.

ASK THE CLASS: What does "oppress" mean? What was the oppression in this story?

RESPECTING ALL GENDERS

The story has a message about equality between genders. Write what each part of the story might stand for.

This part of the story:

Is like:

PERCENTAGES AND FRACTIONS = *Men and women*

THE WAY HALF AND 50% HAVE THE SAME VALUE = _____

USING RUBBERS AS A WEAPON = _____

RUBBING OUT SOMEONE'S PERCENT SIGN AS A JOKE = _____

THE NOTEBOOKS TILTING TO THE SIDE = _____

RESPECTING ALL GENDERS

This part of the story:		Is like:
PERCENTAGES AND FRACTIONS	=	*Men and women*
THE WAY HALF AND 50% HAVE THE SAME VALUE	=	*People of all genders being equal to each other*
USING RUBBERS AS A WEAPON	=	*Using strength or power to mistreat others*
RUBBING OUT SOMEONE'S PERCENT SIGN AS A JOKE	=	*Sexist comments or harassment disguised as a joke*
THE NOTEBOOKS TILTING TO THE SIDE	=	*The harm caused by gender inequality*

LEARNING POINT

WHAT CAN WE SAY ABOUT GENDER EQUALITY?

- People of different genders are like half and 50%: different but equal.
- One group picking on another doesn't make sense and isn't fair, even if it sounds like a joke.

How is gender equality like equality in maths? Match up the story cards (1–5) with the explanation cards (A–E).

STORY CARDS	EXPLANATION CARDS

	STORY CARDS		EXPLANATION CARDS
1	Two numbers can be **DIFFERENT BUT EQUAL**, though not everyone can see it.	A	We each need to check our own behaviour in case we are accidentally getting in the way of gender equality. For example, might something we thought was funny actually have been hurtful? If we see it happening, then, like the Great Infinity, we can be brave and powerful enough to speak up. Doing the right thing is rarely something that people regret.
2	On Mathematica, certain kinds of jokes were **COMMON BUT NOT HARMLESS.**	B	Just like half and 50% have the same value, so do all people, no matter their gender. It's common for people to forget that, but it's obvious when you think about it.
3	One group can end up with **TOO MUCH POWER** (e.g., the Frazzles' rubbers).	C	If something happens every day, you might stop noticing. But just because a joke feels normal doesn't make it harmless. That's how it was for the badly treated numbers on Mathematica, and that's how it is for certain genders. If a game or joke is always targeted at the same group, it isn't funny.
4	In the end, **INEQUALITY IS EVERYONE'S PROBLEM** like it was on Mathematica.	D	When the Frazzles on Mathematica discovered rubbers, they gained power by using them as a weapon. In the old days, physical strength and masculinity dominated other genders in the same way. Now, different kinds of strength are valued equally. We try to make sure that no one group has too much power and have laws to protect equal rights.
5	**IT'S RIGHT TO CALL PEOPLE OUT** on their behaviour, like the Great Infinity did.	E	Eventually, on Mathematica, all the numbers' homes and lives were harmed by the inequality experienced by some. Here on our own planet, inequality is dangerous because of the bad feelings it causes and because it means whole groups of people can't work at their best and contribute their full potential to society.

1 matches with ___ 3 matches with ___ 5 matches with ___
2 matches with ___ 4 matches with ___

RESPECTING ALL GENDERS

EXTENSION ACTIVITIES

Have you ever heard a joke that was hurtful instead of funny? Write the joke on one side of the paper, and the possible harmful effect on the other. Now draw in the weighing scales (coming down on one side or the other) to show if you think the humour outweighed the hurt or the other way around.

Listen to the song "One Love" by Bob Marley and the Wailers. What messages about equality do the lyrics give? Make your own song or rap with lyrics that teach the listener about equal rights.

Write down as many examples as you can of gender inequality from the past (e.g., women could not own a house). Compare notes with a classmate and discuss whether there are any "leftovers" from these historic inequalities in today's society.

ANSWERS for the card matching activity

1 matches with B

2 matches with C

3 matches with D

4 matches with E

5 matches with A

TEACHING NOTES

- **Diversity:** Become familiar with the diverse cultural backgrounds represented within the classroom. Are any protected characteristics represented in the group of learners or in their community? Do all the children feel visible and represented in a positive and inclusive way during the session? Can you use the toolkit to address any issues experienced within the group of learners?

- **Group management:** Carefully manage how groups of learners are formed for the activity to address any issues or concerns.

- **Safeguarding:** Follow your setting's Child Protection and Safeguarding policies and speak with the Designated Safeguarding Lead regarding **any** concerns about a child's welfare: disclosure or indicators of abuse, neglect or exploitation. Signpost to sources of support and help.

- **Policies:** Check your setting's anti-bullying, behaviour and equality policies.

7 Secret or surprise
Voicing concerns

R Relationships education

H Health education

LEARNING POINTS	KEYWORDS
Knowing the difference between planning a nice surprise and keeping a secret is important for personal safety and wellbeing. You should trust your gut feeling when you're asked to keep something secret. If something doesn't feel right and you're worried or feel unsafe, you should ask for support and help. Everyone has the right to their own personal boundaries and privacy. Nobody should be made to feel guilty or shameful.	Secret vs. surprise Healthy / unhealthy relationships Personal boundaries Consent Safety Privacy Choice Rights Autonomy Communication Emotions Concerns Worries Gut feeling Pressure Shame Guilt Support Help

DOI: 10.4324/9781003391654-10

SECRET OR SURPRISE

Read this story aloud to the group, using the prompt questions to encourage active listening.

PART 1

Imagine you're a servant in a large, dusty old palace in Persia, in the days of myths and fairytales. Beautiful tiles cover every inch of the palace walls and floors, and your job is to polish them. You don't mind the work. The tiles sparkle brightly and lift your spirits, even those that line the underground tunnel through which you walk in and out of the palace each day.

But one day, as you're going to work, a tall, dark figure limps out of a doorway right at the tunnel's mid-section. "Name's Grimmstall," it whimpers, shaking your hand. Grimstall seems to have a bad leg. He limps alongside you so pitifully that when he hands you his backpack, you don't mind shouldering it. No sooner have you done so than Grimmstall hands you a note and runs off cackling. In dark writing, the note reads:

Look inside or take me off your shoulders, and you will feel the tunnel crash down in bricks and boulders.

ASK THE CLASS: Do you always have to say yes to grown-ups?

PART 2

There's no sign of Grimmstall the next day or the day after that. You don't dare take the backpack off. But each day, as you pass through the tunnel, it gets heavier, as if the dark figure has added a large stone to its weight.

The backpack rattles a little as you walk, but nobody seems to hear it. "Wait up," you call to your boss, the Head Cleaner, as you make your way to work. "I can't... it's just I..." but before you can get the words out, he slaps you on the back. "Come on, we'll be late," he says as he strides onwards.

ASK THE CLASS: What are some barriers to sharing a problem that you might have?

SECRET OR SURPRISE

Read this story aloud to the group, using the prompt questions to encourage active listening.

PART 3

Twenty days later, the backpack is as heavy as you, and carrying it is starting to hurt. You've begun to limp so badly – as pitifully as Grimmstall himself – that the chief groundsman calls your name. Hoping for a kind word, you lean against the wall and lift your eyes to face him. "Buck up, child," he growls at you. "There's no work here for those who can't walk."

Frantic with worry as you drag yourself through the tunnel that evening on your way home, you shout into the darkness: "Grimstall! What's in this backpack?" A grizzly voice echoes back: "Mind your own business. Questions are bad news."

ASK THE CLASS: Are questions bad?

PART 4

Unable to go on, and ready to face the consequences, the next day you beg a fellow servant for help. You could cry with relief when he offers to meet you at the mouth of the tunnel before heading home for dinner.

That evening, at the mouth of the tunnel, your friend begins to lift the backpack from your shoulders. You hear a great cracking sound, and fling your arms around your head in fear, remembering the dire warning in the note, but nothing falls from above. The screams you can hear are coming from inside the tunnel. They are coming from Grimstall himself, crushed to dust by bricks and boulders as the tunnel's walls come crashing down around him. By the time you and your friend look inside the backpack, it is light as a feather and empty inside.

ASK THE CLASS: What was Grimstall's lie and why might he have told it?

SECRET OR SURPRISE

The story has a message about secrets. Write what each part of the story might stand for.

This part of the story: **Is like:**

THE SERVANT'S BACKPACK = *A secret*

THE MESSAGE ABOUT THE TUNNEL FALLING IN =

_____
_____
_____

THE HEAVY WEIGHT OF THE BACKPACK =

_____
_____
_____

THE FELLOW SERVANT =

_____
_____
_____

THE EMPTY BACKPACK AT THE END =

_____
_____
_____

SECRET OR SURPRISE

This part of the story:		**Is like:**
THE SERVANT'S BACKPACK	=	*A secret*
THE MESSAGE ABOUT THE TUNNEL FALLING IN	=	*Something you might fear will happen if you reveal a secret*
THE HEAVY WEIGHT OF THE BACKPACK	=	*The feeling of worry when you have to keep a secret*
THE FELLOW SERVANT	=	*A friend you can confide in*
THE EMPTY BACKPACK AT THE END	=	*The feeling of relief after asking for help with a secret*

LEARNING POINT

WHAT CAN WE SAY ABOUT SECRETS?

- No one should ask you to carry one around forever.
- You don't have to bear one alone – others can help, but they may not find out unless you tell them.

How is a backpack like a secret? Match up the story cards (1–5) with the explanation cards (A–E).

STORY CARDS	EXPLANATION CARDS

1	**YOU CAN'T TELL WHAT'S INSIDE a backpack just by looking at it.**	A	If you have to carry something for a long time, it can feel as if it gets heavier as your muscles begin to get tired and strained. It can be the same with something you have had to hide for a long time. Feeling unsafe, isolated or worried for can take a toll on your feelings and your mental health.
2	**A backpack can get HEAVIER THE LONGER YOU CARRY IT.**	B	If a heavy backpack was causing you physical harm, a person you trust would help gladly. They wouldn't be angry with you for asking. Neither should it be forbidden to ask for help with a difficult secret. When you share it, things might happen as a result, but that's for grown-ups to worry about. It's never your fault and will never reflect badly on you.
3	**No one should have to carry a backpack WITHOUT PUTTING IT DOWN.**	C	We don't know what's inside someone's backpack or inside their head and heart. If it would help you to have someone else's understanding, you have to open up and let them know.
4	**YOU CAN ASK FOR HELP to lighten the load of a backpack.**	D	We carry a backpack from place to place and then put it down. That's like concealing a surprise (say, a birthday present) for a short time. The difference between a surprise and a secret is that a secret is usually meant to be forever, and that's usually not a good thing. After all, can you think of a good reason that anyone would ask you to carry a backpack around forever?
5	**NO ONE WOULD BE ANGRY IF YOU ASKED FOR HELP with a backpack.**	E	Sharing a physical load can make it much easier to bear. In the same way, sharing a mental load can take the weight off your mind. It's not always easy to ask for help, but when you do, you may start to feel better straight away. Remember that offering help can make you feel good, too!

1 matches with ___ 3 matches with ___ 5 matches with ___
2 matches with ___ 4 matches with ___

SECRET OR SURPRISE

EXTENSION ACTIVITIES

 Ask students to draw a backpack and write down (in private) three things that are in their backpack right now, weighing them down and making them feel worried, angry or ashamed. Outside of the backpack, ask them to write three names of people who might be able to help.

 Listen to "Stand By You" by Rachel Platten and then review the lyrics in small groups. Find three metaphors and say what each one means. What do you think is the main message of the song? Who would you like to say this to? Who might say it to you?

 Memorise the phrase "Excuse me, I need help" in three different languages, and get in pairs to test each other. Now, together, write down three different ways of asking for help, all in the English language. Share your favourite with the group.

ANSWERS for the card matching activity

1 matches with C
2 matches with A
3 matches with D
4 matches with E
5 matches with B

TEACHING NOTES

- **Safeguarding:** Follow your setting's Child Protection and Safeguarding policies and speak with the Designated Safeguarding Lead regarding **any** concerns about a child's welfare: disclosure or indicators of abuse, neglect or exploitation. Signpost to sources of support and help.

- **Confidentiality:** Refer back to the class ground rules to reiterate confidentiality: not sharing personal or private information during the session. Worries and concerns are always valid, so encourage children to share with a trusted adult. Signpost to sources that can support and help.

8 Choosing for my body
Boundaries

R Relationships education

H Health education

LEARNING POINTS	KEYWORDS
Bodily autonomy means knowing that your body belongs to you and that everyone gets to decide about their body for themselves.

You should trust your gut feeling when something doesn't feel right and know where to go to ask for support and help when you're worried or feel unsafe.

Everyone has the right to their own personal boundaries and privacy. Nobody should be made to feel guilty or shameful. | Personal boundaries
Consent
Choice
Rights
Autonomy
Safety
Privacy
Emotions
Concerns
Worries
Gut feeling
Pressure
Shame
Guilt
Report
Support
Help |

DOI: 10.4324/9781003391654-11

CHOOSING FOR MY BODY

PART 1

High up in the heavens, in a place called Mount Olympus, live the Gods of the Human Heart. They are having a feast. At the head of the table sits Courage. Near her are three lesser Gods, their voices raised in argument. Their names are Shame, Fear and Pity; each believes they should be seated at the head of the High Table, first among the Gods.

Lady Courage soon tires of their squabble. Letting her heavenly spoon drop, she glances down on humanity. A girl catches her eye. She's about 11 years old, quite short, with candy floss around her mouth. Her name is Kelly. She is celebrating her birthday with three friends at Fate Kingdom, a theme park famous for its most terrifying ride, the Paralysing Plunge. "I will set you a challenge," says Courage with a smirk to Shame, Pity and Fear. "Any who completes the challenge may take my place at the table." With a flick of her hand, she sends the three lesser gods descending through the clouds, toward earth.

ASK THE CLASS: What do you think the Gods of the Human Heart are meant to be in this story? Courage, shame, pity and fear are all what?

PART 2

Down on Earth, Kelly's eyes are turned upward toward the highest tower in Fate Kingdom. Feet are just visible dangling from the summit, about to take the plunge. All of a sudden, Kelly's eyes mist over. She drifts away from her three friends and, without quite meaning to, she finds herself in the queue for the Paralysing Plunge itself.

It's so high, thinks Kelly. She swallows hard, gives her head a little shake and turns to go. But as she does so, she almost crashes into one of her friends – or someone who looks very like her. She has the same glossy black plait and purple glitter top, but there's something funny about her. With a spiteful look, Kelly's friend says to her, "I thought you'd finally grown up a bit, but fine – off you go, back to the baby rides."

ASK THE CLASS: Which God do you think is pretending to be Kelly's friend: Fear, Pity or Shame?

85

CHOOSING FOR MY BODY

Read this story aloud to the group, using the prompt questions to encourage active listening.

PART 3

Kelly brushes past with a faint frown, and Shame gives an inward howl of rage at his failure to persuade her onto the Paralysing Plunge. The dark-haired girl fades out of sight as fast as she had appeared. No sooner has she gone than, at Kelly's left elbow, is her second friend, wearing a weird expression on his face. Gesturing up at the Plunge, he sneers, "if you don't do it, you're not in our group anymore." Kelly opens her mouth, but her protests are drowned out by her third friend. Appearing out of nowhere, the girl has grabbed Kelly's shoulders and is wailing "Please! I'll be all alone if you don't go on the ride with me!"

ASK THE CLASS: What tactics have the other gods used on Kelly while pretending to be her friends?

PART 4

From the high table up in the clouds, Lady Courage gives a lazy wave of her hand. All of a sudden Kelly's head feels quite clear again. She looks up at the Paralysing Plunge and says in a firm voice, "Stop it, guys. I don't want to do this." But she sees, with a little blink, that she's talking to herself. The other three are nowhere to be seen.

"Hey!" comes a shout from the candyfloss booth. Kelly's friends are walking toward her, back to normal with smiles on their faces. "There you are! You're not going on the Paralysing Plunge are you?" says one. "Rather you than me."

"Nah" said Kelly, pulling a what-was-I-thinking face. "Don't fancy it."

ASK THE CLASS: Which kind of pressure is most persuasive: shame, fear or pity? Does it come from other people or from inside our own heads?

CHOOSING FOR MY BODY

The story has a message about choosing for our bodies. Write what each part of the story might stand for.

This part of the story:

Is like:

A SCARY RIDE IN A THEME PARK   =   *Doing something physical with your body*

THE QUEUE FOR THE SCARY RIDE   =   _____
_____
_____

THE GODS FEAR, PITY AND SHAME   =   _____
_____
_____

THE GODS' DISGUISE AS FRIENDS   =   _____
_____
_____

THE HEAD GOD COURAGE   =   _____
_____

CHOOSING FOR MY BODY

This part of the story:		Is like:
A SCARY RIDE IN A THEME PARK	=	*Doing something physical with your body*
THE QUEUE FOR THE SCARY RIDE	=	*Making a choice for your body that you're not sure about*
THE GODS FEAR, PITY AND SHAME	=	*The feelings you have when you are being pressured*
THE GODS' DISGUISE AS FRIENDS	=	*People pretending to be on your side but not taking care of your feelings*
THE HEAD GOD COURAGE	=	*Understanding that it's your choice no matter what someone else wants*

LEARNING POINT

WHAT CAN WE SAY ABOUT CHOOSING FOR MY BODY?

- You might have mixed feelings and you're not sure what you want, but you should feel completely free to choose.
- Nobody should make you feel bad for the choice you make.

How is a scary ride like choosing for your body? Match up the story cards (1–5) with the explanation cards (A–E).

STORY CARDS **EXPLANATION CARDS**

1 — What you feel about going on a scary ride might be CONFUSING. — **A** — Only you can choose what you do with your body, whether that's going on a scary ride in a theme park or funfair or letting someone else get close to it. You can say "no", or you can say "yes" but change your mind at any moment. So can anyone else.

2 — PRESSURE from other people MIGHT AFFECT YOUR DECISION about a scary ride. — **B** — If you listen carefully to your mind and body, they will tell you what you really want. Try to listen to this "gut feeling." That might be an "icky" or uncomfortable feeling that makes you want to take a step backward or an excited one that makes you feel strong. Once you know, you can trust that feeling and say what you want.

3 — EVERYBODY GETS TO CHOOSE FOR THEMSELVES about a scary ride. — **C** — When faced with something like the Paralysing Plunge, you might feel scared and excited all at once. You might not even be sure if it's a good or a bad feeling. Any choice that involves your body can feel like that, including whether to be close to someone else.

4 — NOBODY SHOULD MAKE YOU FEEL BAD if you want to say no to a scary ride or stop. — **D** — Someone else might try to persuade you to do something, or it might seem that everyone wants to do it. If you feel like the odd one out, it can be embarrassing to admit that you don't want to. Remember, you don't know what other people are truly thinking and feeling, but you can listen to your own feelings.

5 — You could TRUST YOUR FEELINGS AND SPEAK UP if you didn't want to go on a scary ride. — **E** — Even though it's your body, another person might try to make you feel ashamed, anxious or even sorry for them if you say "no" to something. It's not your problem if other people are disappointed. Having control over your own body is more important.

1 matches with ___ 3 matches with ___ 5 matches with ___
2 matches with ___ 4 matches with ___

CHOOSING FOR MY BODY

EXTENSION ACTIVITIES

 Watch the short video by Aardman called "Consent" (directed by Tim Ruffle): https://www.aardman.com/latest-news/aardman-consent-film -opcc

In groups, discuss what happens when two people want different things?

 Open your favourite book and look for an example of someone's "outer voice" (something they say out loud) and their "inner voice" (what they are thinking or feeling inside). What is the difference in how each is presented? Think of ways you can tell what someone's inner voice is saying in real life, even if they haven't spoken.

 Pair up and play four rounds of "rock, paper, scissors" with your partner. Then play four more rounds really slowly and carefully, looking for clues in your partner's last move and how they are behaving. Talk about how you know what someone else is thinking.

ANSWERS for the card matching activity

1 matches with C

2 matches with D

3 matches with A

4 matches with E

5 matches with B

TEACHING NOTES

- **Safeguarding:** Follow your setting's Child Protection and Safeguarding policies and speak with the Designated Safeguarding Lead regarding **any** concerns about a child's welfare: disclosure or indicators of abuse, neglect or exploitation. Signpost to sources of support and help.

- **Confidentiality:** Refer back to the class ground rules to reiterate confidentiality: not sharing personal or private information during the session. Worries and concerns are always valid so encourage children to share with a trusted adult. Signpost to sources that can support and help.

9 My amazing body
Private body parts

R
Relationships education

H
Health education

Sc
Science

LEARNING POINTS	KEYWORDS
Bodily autonomy means knowing that your body belongs to you and that everyone gets to decide about their body for themselves.

Knowing the vocabulary for private body parts means that you're able to have bodily autonomy and ask for support and help when you need it.

Using correct terminology helps safeguard against ill health and abuse.

We can all appreciate our amazing bodies for what they can do. Nothing about our bodies needs to be shameful. | My body belongs to me
Autonomy
Boundaries
Rights
Safety
Privacy
Taboo
Worries
Concerns
Gut feeling
Report
Support
Help
Correct terminology:
    Female: Vulva, vagina, clitoris, labia
    Male: Penis, glans, foreskin, testicles, scrotum |

DOI: 10.4324/9781003391654-12

MY AMAZING BODY

Read this story aloud to the group, using the prompt questions to encourage active listening.

PART 1

Picture a beautiful island holiday resort. One morning, all the people that live and work there wake up to discover that a box full of machines has arrived, as if from nowhere. The machines are small, smooth and shiny. Once they've figured out how to turn them on and what all the funny buttons are for, everyone on the island finds them very useful. The chefs can find new recipes. The hotel bosses can calculate complicated sums. The entertainment manager can type up the day's activities.

Before long, everyone on the island is using their machines every day. But for some reason, they feel a little ashamed of how the machines have changed their lives. The islanders don't like to use them or even talk about them in front of each other, and they certainly never give any part of their machines a name.

ASK THE CLASS: What do you think the machines are?

PART 2

Alice, the island locksmith, isn't like the other islanders. No sooner has she taken her machine home than she begins to investigate it, piece by piece. She picks apart a row of buttons and finds out how pressing them makes a letter appear. Those buttons, she calls "keys." She experiments with how fast you can whizz the arrow across the screen, using a flat patch that she calls "the mousepad." She sees how the holes in the side connect to the dangly bit. She calls that "the charger."

Alice tries to get her fellow islanders to share these names, but each refuses, some covering their ears and some shrieking with embarrassment. "Why not?" asks Alice. "They crack apart when you do that!" says the pastry chef in a hushed whisper. "The magic will fail!" cries her friend, the housekeeper. "Just... shush!" cries the groundswoman.

ASK THE CLASS: What do you think causes rumours and misunderstandings like this?

MY AMAZING BODY

Read this story aloud to the group, using the prompt questions to encourage active listening.

PART 3

After a year or two, the islanders' machines begin to show signs of wear and tear. *Well, we do use them every day*, reasons Alice. Sometimes it goes even further than the odd scratch. One day, Alice notices that although the pastry chef still carries her machine everywhere (hidden in its cover, of course, as is proper), she has completely stopped using it.

Alice asks one day why that is. "Oh, nothing wrong, nothing wrong, my friend," the chef responds heartily. "I've got one and that's that. Can't complain." But that night, at the darkest hour, Alice's doorbell rings. She finds Chef standing on the step, sobbing. "Help me! My... thing... it won't work. I don't know what to do."

ASK THE CLASS: What is it called when people don't like to talk about something?

PART 4

"Listen," Alice puts her hand on Chef's shoulder. "These machines, I know they're amazing, maybe even magic, but that doesn't mean we can't look under their lids, give things a name and understand how they work." After a cup of tea and some persuasion, she gets permission from Chef to unzip the case and begins to examine the machine. Alice tells Chef about all the different parts as she works. Five minutes later, she shuts the lid and says, "I think the headphone port just needs a clean," at which her friend lets out a sharp breath of relief. Alice blows into one of the little holes, plugs in a wire, and the machine comes whirring back to life.

ASK THE CLASS: Why didn't the Chef know what to do?

MY AMAZING BODY

The story has a message about understanding our bodies. Write what each part of the story might stand for.

This part of the story: **Is like:**

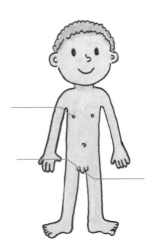

SOMEBODY'S PERSONAL COMPUTER = *A person's body*

THE AMAZING THINGS COMPUTERS CAN DO FOR US = _____
_____
_____

THE PARTS OF A COMPUTER THAT MANY PEOPLE CAN'T NAME = _____
_____
_____

THE PEOPLE'S EMBARRASSMENT & CONFUSION ABOUT THEIR COMPUTERS = _____
_____
_____
_____

AN EXPERT WHO CAN FIX YOUR COMPUTER = _____
_____
_____

MY AMAZING BODY

This part of the story:		**Is like:**
SOMEBODY'S PERSONAL COMPUTER	=	*A person's body*
THE AMAZING THINGS COMPUTERS CAN DO FOR US	=	*The amazing things a human body can do*
THE PARTS OF A COMPUTER THAT MANY PEOPLE CAN'T NAME	=	*Parts of a human body whose names people often don't know*
THE PEOPLE'S EMBARRASSMENT & CONFUSION ABOUT THEIR COMPUTERS	=	*Taboos about the human body*
AN EXPERT WHO CAN FIX YOUR COMPUTER	=	*A trusted adult, doctor or nurse*

LEARNING POINT

WHAT CAN WE SAY ABOUT OUR BODIES?

- Like computers, our bodies are complicated but amazing.
- Understanding them properly and knowing what each part is called helps us to appreciate and take care of what we have.

95

SUPPORT MATERIAL

How is a computer like a human body? Match up the story cards (1–5) with the explanation cards (A–E).

STORY CARDS	EXPLANATION CARDS

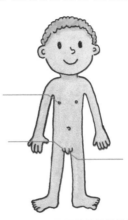

1	My computer is AMAZING and it WORKS LIKE MAGIC.	A	Do you know the difference between a hard drive and a USB port? How about a vulva and a vagina? Even if some private body parts have nicknames, it's important to know the correct words, too. If we can't name them, how can we take care of them and ask for help clearly when we need it?
2	My computer NEEDS TO BE TREATED CAREFULLY.	B	The same rules about personal property also apply to personal space. It wouldn't be right to grab or even touch someone's computer without their permission. It's up to them to say what happens to it. If they want you to touch it (for example, to ask for help with it), they'll ask. It's the same with bodies.
3	My computer HAS LOTS OF PARTS WITH TRICKY NAMES – some inside, some outside.	C	Like computers, human bodies have hundreds of complicated little parts. They are not always easy to fix and doing so takes a lot of expertise. So, they need to be appreciated, respected and cared for properly.
4	Nobody gets to TOUCH my personal computer UNLESS I SAY THEY CAN.	D	It takes many years of study to understand even the basics of how a computer or a human body works. Both are so complicated that it can feel like magic. It's a miracle that our bodies work the way they do and that's something we can be thankful for.
5	My computer might be personal, but it's NOT A DARK SECRET.	E	Someone's personal computer might usually be kept in a case or a bag, but there doesn't need to be any big secret or mystery about it. You might feel the same way about your body. Even though parts of it are private, that doesn't mean that we should feel ashamed of them and not name them or ask for help with them.

1 matches with ___   3 matches with ___   5 matches with ___

2 matches with ___   4 matches with ___

MY AMAZING BODY

EXTENSION ACTIVITIES

 Draw a simple Venn diagram, labelling each circle MALE and FEMALE, and the section in the middle BOTH. Challenge yourself to write as many of the correct names for private body parts in each section as you can and compare with a partner afterward. (Remember: there are lots of parts of the body that we consider private, not just the genitals).

 Play a game of Taboo. Each person writes a hard-to-guess body part on a piece of paper. Take turns to pull one out of a hat and describe what it is without using the word itself or using gestures.

 Write a thank you letter or poem to your body. It should describe what you appreciate about it and feel thankful for.

ANSWERS for the card matching activity

1 matches with D
2 matches with C
3 matches with A
4 matches with B
5 matches with E

TEACHING NOTES

- **Correct safeguarding terminology for private body parts:** It is not unusual for children to use or suggest colloquial or inappropriate language about private body parts without meaning to be rude. Avoid reprimanding children if they use incorrect terminology before being introduced to the correct ones. Explain that adults often find it difficult to use or teach the correct terminology because they didn't learn this themselves when they were younger. Being able to use correct terminology about private body parts supports children's bodily autonomy and is a safeguarding measure against ill health and sexual abuse.

- **Safeguarding:** Follow your setting's Child Protection and Safeguarding policies and speak with the Designated Safeguarding Lead regarding **any** concerns about a child's welfare: disclosure or indicators of abuse, neglect or exploitation. Signpost to sources of support and help.

10 Changing bodies
Puberty

R Relationships education

H Health education

Sc Science

LEARNING POINTS	KEYWORDS
Puberty is the stage in life when children start to develop into adults. It is important to know about puberty changes before they happen. Puberty is a normal and healthy part of life with many different emotional, physical and social changes. Although some puberty changes can feel strange or unsettling it is an exciting time for learning about oneself and others and for becoming more independent. Having people around you who you trust and knowing where to ask questions is an important part of keeping happy, healthy and safe during puberty.	Puberty Adolescence Teenager Hormones Emotional Physical Social Changes Privacy Boundaries Information Support Help

DOI: 10.4324/9781003391654-13

Read this story aloud to the group, using the prompt questions to encourage active listening.

PART 1

"Thank you," said Bennie the caterpillar politely when offered a tasty leaf, "but I'm just not that hungry." From all over the rose plant, dozens of eyes turned his way. "Not even a nice petal?" said a big fat cabbage moth kid that looked almost fully grown. Little Cabbage Looper stared at Bennie in amusement. "You can't be serious? *All* caterpillars are hungry!"

Bennie's stomach betrayed him with a loud rumble. The truth was, he was so hungry he could eat a holly bush. It's just that... he liked being a caterpillar. He liked his powerful, wriggly body, and he really liked it being green. He liked having 16 legs and, above all, he liked having every single one of them stuck safely to a leaf. Preferably out of sight on the underside of a leaf.

ASK THE CLASS: What do we know about caterpillars?

PART 2

Much as Bennie liked things just the way they were, certain things had begun to happen. He'd outgrown his skin five times since he joined this rose. And each time he'd grown a new skin, it had come out a little bit less green. He wasn't blending in like he used to. Yesterday, a ladybird had waved to him from right over the other side of the garden!

Looper saw Bennie crawl underneath the largest leaf on the rose bush and clamp his mouth firmly shut. "Bennie," he ventured. "I think it's time, isn't it?"

"Time for what?" said Bennie. "No, it isn't." But his back was beginning to tingle. He could feel something going on, deep inside.

ASK THE CLASS: If Bennie were human, what age do you think he would be?

Read this story aloud to the group, using the prompt questions to encourage active listening.

PART 3

Looper waved to Bennie's Mama, calling her in to land. You could spot her a mile off: the biggest, loudest, brightest insect in the garden.

She landed in a flash of blue, purple and red and waited patiently for Bennie to talk. "Mama," he began after a pause. His voice grew to a wail, "The sky is so bright, and the world is so big."

"Yes!" said Mama, flushed with joy, her face upturned. "The sky *is* bright, and the world *is* big." And then she spread her magnificent wings so wide that Bennie could see nothing but his leaf and his Mama. The world dimmed, and the chirping muted just enough for Bennie's head to clear. "Now spin," said Mama.

ASK THE CLASS: What is it that Bennie and his mama feel differently about?

PART 4

After seven days of silence and peace, Bennie woke up inside his silk cocoon and began to squeeze himself out. It felt strange – sometimes uncomfortable – but it didn't hurt. Mama was there, waiting. "Spread your wings, my love. We need to hurry." Bennie looked up and saw a bird circling close overhead. He made a hasty dive underneath his leaf, but his body was huge and cumbersome, and he fell off. "Spread your wings," Mama said again. Carefully, from the earth below, Bennie unfolded himself. The bird in the sky was poised on the brink of a dive. Together, in a flash of colour, the two butterflies took flight into the night sky.

ASK THE CLASS: What is good about Bennie's changes?

CHANGING BODIES

The story has a message about puberty. Write what each part of the story might stand for.

This part of the story: **Is like:**

A CATERPILLAR = *A growing child*

ALL THE LEAVES A
CATERPILLAR MUST EAT = _____
_____
_____

A CATERPILLAR GOING
INTO ITS CHRYSALIS = _____
_____
_____

A BUTTERFLY = _____
_____
_____

A BUTTERFLY'S ABILITY TO
FLY = _____
_____
_____

CHANGING BODIES

This part of the story:		**Is like:**
A CATERPILLAR	=	*A growing child*
ALL THE LEAVES A CATERPILLAR MUST EAT	=	*All the energy that a growing child needs to develop*
A CATERPILLAR GOING INTO ITS CHRYSALIS	=	*A child entering puberty*
A BUTTERFLY	=	*A fully developed adult*
A BUTTERFLY'S ABILITY TO FLY	=	*The joy and freedom that becoming an adult can bring*

LEARNING POINT

WHAT CAN WE SAY ABOUT PUBERTY?

- Children are like caterpillars because they change when they turn into grown-ups.
- These changes are normal and inevitable; they are exciting, even if they take a while to get used to.

How is a caterpillar like a child? Match up the story cards (1–5) with the explanation cards (A–E).

STORY CARDS	EXPLANATION CARDS

1	A caterpillar **DOESN'T LOOK QUITE THE SAME WHEN IT'S GROWN-UP.**	A — Caterpillars spin themselves a safe cocoon out of silk while they develop into butterflies. Our friends and family can act as our "cocoon" as we change into adults. Like butterflies, we develop our "true colours" (our personality) as adolescents. This can be interesting but sometimes awkward; your new self will take a bit of getting used to.
2	The changes that happen to a caterpillar are **SURPRISING BUT NORMAL.**	B — They might not be as easily visible as the changes that happen to a caterpillar, but humans do experience lots of changes as they grow into adulthood. These include physical changes: body shape, body hair, skin and private body parts. Emotional and social changes happen too, including moods, feelings, friendships and how we become attracted to other people.
3	A caterpillar **CHANGES TO HELP IT THRIVE IN THE WIDER WORLD.**	C — Even though the change from caterpillar to butterfly is a dramatic one, it is natural and meant to happen. The changes that happen to us during puberty are also natural and normal. There is nothing to be alarmed about; every adult has gone through it.
4	A caterpillar is very hungry because what happens to it **TAKES A LOT OF ENERGY.**	D — Caterpillars are famously hungry; they can eat so much that they double in size in one day! Puberty is a bit slower than that, but while it's going on, humans also need a lot of food and rest to help them grow and get used to all the changes.
5	A caterpillar **NEEDS SAFETY AND PRIVACY WHILE IT DEVELOPS.**	E — Caterpillars change into butterflies for good reasons: flying helps them get enough to eat and escape predators. And the changes that happen to us during puberty also equip us to meet the challenges and opportunities of the adult world. Puberty is our bodies getting ready for us to fall in love and make families of our own if we want to.

1 matches with ___   3 matches with ___   5 matches with ___
2 matches with ___   4 matches with ___

CHANGING BODIES

EXTENSION ACTIVITIES

 Draw or paint your own butterfly. Inside each spot, write one of the physical, emotional or social changes that will happen during puberty to "make you you" (e.g., give you your spots). Alternatively, draw a human body outline and label it with those changes. Compare it with others' and see what you can learn from each other.

 Imagine you are a child who has been told nothing about puberty. Write an email to your doctor describing what is happening without using any technical or scientific terms. Next, imagine you are the doctor and write an email back reassuring the child. Vote for the "best doctor" at the end.

 Draw a butterfly's cocoon on the whiteboard and the question: *What help will I need during puberty?* Write ideas around it (or on post-its to stick around it). Think about the people you might need to ask for this help.

ANSWERS for the card matching activity

1 matches with B

2 matches with C

3 matches with E

4 matches with D

5 matches with A

TEACHING NOTES

- **Puberty stages:** The children in class will be approaching puberty at different times. Be mindful of children who have started puberty before others or children who are yet to start growing and changing. Both can feel "different" or "stand out" during the session.

- **Diversity:** Become familiar with the diverse cultural backgrounds represented within the classroom. These may affect how much the children learn at home about puberty. Likewise, children with older siblings will know more about puberty changes than others.

- **Safeguarding:** Follow your setting's Child Protection and Safeguarding policies and speak with the Designated Safeguarding Lead regarding **any** concerns about a child's welfare: disclosure or indicators of abuse, neglect or exploitation. Signpost to sources of support and help.

11 Wet dreams
Nocturnal emissions

LEARNING POINTS	KEYWORDS

A normal part of puberty is for the body to make hormones that ready the sexual anatomy to reproduce when you're an adult – this includes wet dreams.
 	
In a male body, wet dreams are when sperm is released from the testicles, then fluids are added to make semen that leaves the penis through an erection and ejaculation. In a female body, the clitoris enlarges and the vagina becomes lubricated.
 	
Wet dreams often occur at night during sleep.
 	
Wet dreams happen more often for some people than for others but is perfectly normal and nothing to be worried or ashamed about.
	Puberty
	Hormones
	Correct terminology
	Sexual anatomy
	Reproduction
	Wet dreams
	Correct terminology:
	   Male: Penis, testicles, sperm, semen, erection, ejaculation
	   Female: Clitoris enlarges, vagina lubricates
	Normal
	Privacy
	Communication
	Support
	Help

DOI: 10.4324/9781003391654-14

WET DREAMS

Read this story aloud to the group, using the prompt questions to encourage active listening.

PART 1

Imagine you're a creature who wakes up in its cave one day with a feeling of trepidation. Did it happen again last night? You don't always know straight away. Stretching yourself awake, you give your aching wings a shake (they have grown so large that you've ended up sleeping on one).

You flick your tail, and it bumps against the end of your little cave – a cave that used to suit you just fine when you were small. You pluck up the courage to check the bundle of straw by your head. It is singed to a crisp. So, it did happen. "Oh, come on," you groan, reproaching yourself. You're lucky you didn't burn to a cinder in your sleep. Unsure what to do with the blackened straw, you head outside.

ASK THE CLASS: This creature breathed fire by accident in the night. What kind of creature do you think it is?

PART 2

You chomp down a couple of mice and, with a short, sharp roar to your parents, you take off on your morning expedition.

You've only been able to fly for a few weeks, and it's one thing about the new you that you truly, unconditionally love. It makes you feel strong and powerful, and it's letting you explore the countryside – a vast landscape of which, until now, you've only ever seen a single face of a single mountain.

You've been in the sky for 10 minutes when you spot something so startling you nearly lose your wing stroke. Standing outside a cave just like your own are two creatures that look, amazingly, just like your own family!

ASK THE CLASS: Why has the creature only just discovered that there are others out there like it?

WET DREAMS

Read this story aloud to the group, using the prompt questions to encourage active listening.

PART 3

In a fluster, you land, breathing carefully through your nostrils so that nothing embarrassing happens. You don't want to blow it. You mustn't let ANYTHING out of your mouth – not so much as a spark.

You say to them, "I'm Marmorok," which means "Great Lizard" in the ancient language. "We're Marmorok too," they laugh.

That's when you feel that thing welling up inside you. You clamp your big jaw shut, but you can't stop that building feeling. Without another word, you turn around and take off into the sky.

ASK THE CLASS: Why is the creature embarrassed?

PART 4

You're only a few metres up when the kindly couple calls you back down. You want to talk to someone about what you just felt – what sometimes happens in your sleep – but you couldn't possibly. Then again, you can't carry on like this. You make them promise not to laugh and tell them the whole truth. "It... it happens when I'm asleep," you finish up with a blush. "I don't even know till I wake up."

The larger of the two nods sympathetically. "You'll learn to control it."

They give you a few tips, and then, grinning, say, "look what you can do when you know how!" The two creatures shyly offer up a plate, and on it is something you've never seen before. It's meat, but it's all brown and charred and it smells delicious!

ASK THE CLASS: What is the upside (the benefit) of what the creature can now do?

WET DREAMS

The story has a message about wet dreams. Write what each part of the story might stand for.

This part of the story:

Is like:

THE DRAGON BREATHING FIRE IN ITS SLEEP	=	*A wet dream*
THE DRAGON'S SINGED STRAW	=	_____ _____ _____
THE DRAGON'S FEELINGS ABOUT ACCIDENTALLY BREATHING FIRE	=	_____ _____ _____ _____
REALISING THAT OTHER DRAGONS EXIST	=	_____ _____ _____
A DRAGON BEING ABLE TO USE ITS NEW POWER TO COOK MEAT	=	_____ _____ _____

WET DREAMS

This part of the story:		Is like:
THE DRAGON BREATHING FIRE IN ITS SLEEP	=	*A wet dream*
THE DRAGON'S SINGED STRAW	=	*A marked or stained bedsheet (males only)*
THE DRAGON'S FEELINGS ABOUT ACCIDENTALLY BREATHING FIRE	=	*Someone being embarrassed and unsure of what to do after a wet dream*
REALISING THAT OTHER DRAGONS EXIST	=	*Someone realising that having wet dreams is normal*
A DRAGON BEING ABLE TO USE ITS NEW POWER TO COOK MEAT	=	*A grown-up human being able to fall in love, have sex and reproduce*

LEARNING POINT

WHAT CAN WE SAY ABOUT WET DREAMS?

- Wet dreams are like a dragon finding out it can breathe fire because it can be surprising and hard to control.
- Even though it can be awkward and troublesome, it's normal and means good things.

How is a dragon breathing fire like a human having a wet dream? Match up the story cards (1–5) with the explanation cards (A–E).

STORY CARDS

EXPLANATION CARDS

	STORY CARDS		EXPLANATION CARDS
1	**A dragon is SUDDENLY ABLE TO DO A NEW THING when it breathes fire.**	A	We all know that a dragon can breathe fire, but until it gets this ability under control, this could mean some big challenges! In the same way, if a wet dream leaves a wet patch for males this can feel like a problem. On the other hand, wet dreams usually feel good and point to a healthy body.
2	**A dragon would be TAKEN BY SURPRISE if it were suddenly able to breathe fire.**	B	For a dragon, breathing fire is perfectly natural. So are wet dreams; they're very common and completely normal. That doesn't mean you'll always find it easy to talk about. But the adults around you will always rather that you come to them with a problem than struggle in silence.
3	**For a dragon, breathing fire is A SIGN THAT A NEW PHASE OF LIFE IS POSSIBLE.**	C	All animals change as they grow up, and sometimes this brings new abilities. For humans born with testes, at puberty, they begin to be able to ejaculate (when semen comes out of the end of the penis). This can happen during sleep – what we call a wet dream. People with vulva may also find the clitoris enlarges and the vagina becomes lubricated during a wet dream.
4	**For a dragon, breathing fire would BRING GOOD THINGS BUT ALSO PRESENT PROBLEMS.**	D	It might not be quite as dramatic as breathing fire, but as a wet dream happens unintentionally during sleep, it can come as a surprise. The first time this happens, it might be a bit of a shock, but it is not a sign of anything being wrong.
5	**Fire-breathing is NATURAL BUT DIFFICULT TO TALK ABOUT for a dragon.**	E	The day a dragon learned to breathe fire, many new possibilities would open up for it. Just like that, wet dreams are part of several exciting changes that happen when you grow and develop. They show that your sexual reproductive system is becoming mature. Your body is getting ready in case you want to have a baby one day.

1 matches with ___   3 matches with ___   5 matches with ___

2 matches with ___   4 matches with ___

WET DREAMS

EXTENSION ACTIVITIES

 Write two lists, one for males and one for females, describing what happens when each experiences a wet dream (using the correct words for private body parts). Discuss similarities and differences between the two lists.

 Watch a video about voluntary vs involuntary actions (check suitability for the age/stage of the group of learners). Afterward, ask groups to list four involuntary actions and for each one, explain why it benefits the human body. Make sure wet dreams/nocturnal emissions are included on the list.

 On post-it notes, write as many tactics as you can for making an awkward conversation less awkward (for example, "have a chat in the car when you don't have direct eye contact"). Combine your tactics with a classmate, and together, prioritise your favourites by arranging them in a diamond shape with the best at the top and the worst at the bottom.

ANSWERS for the card matching activity

1 matches with C

2 matches with D

3 matches with E

4 matches with A

5 matches with B

TEACHING NOTES

- **Wet dreams can happen to anyone in puberty:** If children learn that wet dreams only apply to boys (just like teaching about menstruation only to girls), this carries the risk of assigning "pleasure" to males and "hardship" to females. Changes in puberty affect the body's response to hormonal and sexual stimulation in both male and female bodies.

- **Masturbation:** Children may associate learning about wet dreams with "masturbation" and "exploring sexuality" and may ask questions to which the answers may be defined as sex education. Check how your setting's RSHE policy defines sex education, whether it is part of RSHE at primary level and the guidance in place for dealing with children's questions. You could invite children to pose their questions anonymously in a Question Box and prep your answers for a dedicated Q&A session.

- **Safeguarding:** Follow your setting's Child Protection and Safeguarding policies and speak with the Designated Safeguarding Lead regarding **any** concerns about a child's welfare: disclosure or indicators of abuse, neglect or exploitation. Signpost to sources of support and help.

12 Periods
Menstruation

LEARNING POINTS	KEYWORDS
Both females and males need to learn about the menstrual cycle to understand human reproduction. Having this knowledge enables us to support those who have periods to manage the physical and emotional responses they experience.	Menstrual cycle Hormones Ovaries Eggs Fallopian Tubes Womb/Uterus Embryo Lining shedding Menstruation / Period
Females normally start their periods between the age of 10 and 15 (it can start as early as 8 or as late as 17). Periods can be irregular to start with but eventually occur on average every 28 days.	*Physical responses*: cramps, sore breasts, bloating, cravings *Emotional responses*: pride, joy, irritability, mood swings
During the menstrual cycle hormones release an egg from one ovary. The egg travels through the fallopian tube to the womb (uterus) where a lining of blood and fluids has developed to support a possible pregnancy.	Pads Tampons Period pants Cups Information Support Help
When the egg isn't fertilised by sperm (from a male), the lining is shed from the womb and passed through the vagina to the vulva as a period.	
A period lasts for approximately 3-5 days. Females manage their period by using pads, tampons or reusable products.	

DOI: 10.4324/9781003391654-15

PERIODS

Read this story aloud to the group, using the prompt questions to encourage active listening.

PART 1

Today we travel to a faraway hotel in the most remote reaches of outer space. This special hotel happens to belong to the High Commander of the universe. It is decorated entirely in red and pink, just the way the High Commander likes it. Its beds are dressed in the softest cotton available in the galaxy to please the High Commander. The rooms are padded and soundproofed for maximum comfort. In fact, the hotel must comply with every one of the High Commander's 6,017 precise rules and regulations.

ASK THE CLASS: What is the High Commander very particular about?

PART 2

So far, the High Commander has come to stay a total of, well, zero times, but you would never think it to look at the place. The staff of 400 robots maintains the hotel in perfect condition, without fail. Every 28 days, the robots on each corridor get a message from Housekeeping HQ on their walkie talkies: *INITIATE REFURBISHMENT*. Beds are changed, pillows are fluffed. So, they stay untouched and pristine, until 28 days later, when refurbishment begins all over again.

Robot 632, the most hardworking and capable in the hotel, is responsible for the most important room: the Commander's Suite. Every four weeks, like clockwork, Robot 632 carries last month's cotton cushions and blankets down the long corridors and ejects them into space. He replaces the furnishings, smoothing and plumping as he goes, dreading what the High Commander would say if they one day encountered a spike or a lump.

ASK THE CLASS: Why do the robots keep replacing the bedding?

PERIODS

Read this story aloud to the group, using the prompt questions to encourage active listening.

PART 3

It's day 28, and Robot 632 is up early and ready, but today, something strange happens. The message from Housekeeping HQ never comes through. *Initiate Refurbishment*, Robot 632 mutters to himself, distressed. We'll be punished, he thinks, joining the many staff robots that are wheeling around the hotel in disarray. Without thinking, he winds up at the door to the Commander's Suite with a bundle of fresh cotton. But three burly sentries are blocking the door. "No entry," says the very burliest. "This room is occupied by none other than the High Commander."

ASK THE CLASS: Why didn't the robots need to change the rooms today?

PART 4

Robot 632 cowers away from the door. He's almost half a day late to service the room. Will the High Commander's pillows be flat, or – heavens forbid – dusty? The burliest sentry bears down on him with her hands outstretched, but, to his astonishment, she gives a polite smile and pins a shiny medal to his overalls. "For loyal service," she declares. That's when the robot notices a high-tech metal chair outside the room. The sentry explains that the High Commander's bones are as brittle as glass. Their skin can't be exposed to the light. In short, they need a lot of care and protection. "So, thank you for all the care you've taken over the years," finishes the Sentry. "It means a lot to the High Commander."

ASK THE CLASS: Why did the High Commander have so many fussy rules about the hotel, after all?

PERIODS

The story has a message about periods. Write what each part of the story might stand for.

This part of the story:

Is like:

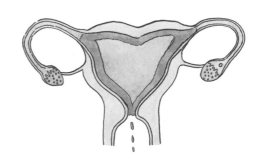

THE HOTEL ROOM = *A womb (uterus)*

THE RED CUSHIONS AND PILLOWS MADE OF SOFTEST COTTON = _____

HOUSEKEEPING CHANGING THE BEDDING EVERY 28 DAYS = _____

THE WALKIE TALKIES USED BY THE ROBOT HOUSEKEEPERS = _____

THE HIGH COMMANDER = _____

PERIODS

This part of the story:		Is like:
THE HOTEL ROOM	=	*A womb (uterus)*
THE RED CUSHIONS AND PILLOWS MADE OF SOFTEST COTTON	=	*The lining of the womb*
HOUSEKEEPING CHANGING THE BEDDING EVERY 28 DAYS	=	*A period: the 28-day menstrual cycle that refreshes the womb lining*
THE WALKIE TALKIES USED BY THE ROBOT HOUSEKEEPERS	=	*The hormones that carry messages around the human body*
THE HIGH COMMANDER	=	*A growing baby with a fragile body*

LEARNING POINT

WHAT CAN WE SAY ABOUT PERIODS?

- A womb is like a hotel: it needs to be just right for a baby to grow in there.
- Periods are like pillows or cushions that need to be changed regularly to provide a good, safe place for a baby.

How is a hotel like a womb? Match up the story cards (1–5) with the explanation cards (A–E).

STORY CARDS	EXPLANATION CARDS

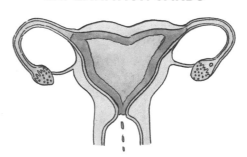

1 — **The hotel room has COMFY, PLUMP RED CUSHIONS AND PILLOWS.**

A — In a hotel, the bedclothes and cushions are taken away down the corridor and changed to keep them fresh. It's the same in a human body; regularly and roughly every 28 days, the soft lining of the womb (uterus) breaks down and leaves the body through the vagina (which is like a corridor to the outside world). We call that a "period".

2 — **The hotel room must be WELL MAINTAINED FOR ITS IMPORTANT GUEST.**

B — Imagine hotel staff all talking into their walkie talkies, passing orders from place to place. In our bodies, hormones do that job; they travel around in the body, carrying messages that trigger changes (for example, triggering a period). During puberty, it can take a while for hormones to settle down into a rhythm.

3 — **The soft cushions and pillows are CHANGED REGULARLY in the hotel room.**

C — In a fancy hotel, staff have to make sure everything is just right inside each room for their guests. Everything needs to be right inside a womb (uterus), too. Its soft, spongy lining provides cushioning and nourishment for an embryo (a collection of cells that will grow into a baby).

4 — **The hotel has a SYSTEM TO PASS AROUND MESSAGES about "housekeeping" work.**

D — In a hotel, staff don't change the beds if there is a guest in the room. And that's the same inside a womb (uterus). If an embryo (a collection of cells that will grow into a baby) takes its place inside a womb, pregnancy begins, and the cycle of renewing the lining is paused.

5 — **If a GUEST IS INSIDE the room, the soft cushions and pillows DON'T GET CHANGED.**

E — The womb (uterus) has a soft, spongy lining made up of cells like any other tissue in the human body. You can think of this like a soft, dark hotel room with plenty of soft furnishings.

1 matches with ___   3 matches with ___   5 matches with ___
2 matches with ___   4 matches with ___

PERIODS

EXTENSION ACTIVITIES

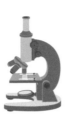

Draw two circles. In one, write and draw the stages of the menstrual cycle. Now think of another example of a cycle in nature (for example, a weather cycle or the water cycle) and draw this in the second circle. Which part of each cycle would you describe as "degeneration" (things breaking down) and which as "renewal" (things being made new again)?

Imagine a girl starting her very first period while at school. Discuss and write down the different things she needs to feel safe, comforted and comfortable. Then compare your notes with others to see what you can learn.

Make a menstrual cycle bracelet with 28 beads or threads: white to represent days of the menstrual cycle with no bleeding, red to represent days with bleeding and one blue to represent ovulation around Day 14. Give the bracelet to a woman or girl as a symbol of solidarity.

ANSWERS for the card matching activity

1 matches with E

2 matches with C

3 matches with A

4 matches with B

5 matches with D

TEACHING NOTES

- **Puberty stages:** The females in class will be approaching puberty at different times. Some may already have started their periods. They may feel "different" or "stand out" during the session, or they may feel proud and happy to share their experience.

- **Diversity:** Become familiar with the diverse cultural backgrounds represented within the classroom. These may affect how much the children learn at home about periods. Likewise, children with older siblings may know more about periods than others.

- **Your context:** Familiarise yourself with the facilities in your setting that will support someone on their period:

  - Toilet facilities including special bins for period products

  - Emergency products for managing an unexpected period

13 Love
Romantic relationships

LEARNING POINTS	KEYWORDS
A normal and healthy part of growing up is to experience attraction and love for other people.	Love Falling in love Having a crush Fancying someone Attraction Romance Mutual LGBT Different emotions Communication Falling out of love Rejection Respect Boundaries Consent Support Help
Having a crush or being in love can feel both great and confusing at the same time.	
Expressing your feelings about being attracted to or not attracted to someone can be difficult. You may be worried about being rejected or hurting someone's feelings.	
Having respect for other people's boundaries while understanding and expressing your own is a healthy and safe response.	
If you feel worried or confused about love and attraction, you should always talk to someone you trust.	

DOI: 10.4324/9781003391654-16

LOVE

Read this story aloud to the group, using the prompt questions to encourage active listening.

PART 1

Imagine yourself in a lush garden, surrounded by colourful flowers. Three bees whirr past you in a rush. If you could speak their language, you'd hear that today is a special day: it's the Annual Nectar Festival. Every year on this day, the flowers bloom, bringing the garden alive with colour, to attract their perfect bee. And every year, each bee follows its nose, bringing the garden alive with the sound of buzzing, to find its soulmate.

When a bee meets a flower, it accepts the gift of nectar. In the months that follow, a process takes place that is so mysterious no human can ever fully understand it. Slowly but surely, that nectar transforms into something sweet and precious – something golden and good.

ASK THE CLASS: What is made from the nectar after all those months?

PART 2

In the garden, Buzz Lopez trails behind his siblings – two confident older bees – listening in as they argue. Pedro, the oldest, is rowdy but good-natured. He swats at a huge Lily, buzzing like mad around its deep pink petals. Lupita interrupts with a showy yawn. "Yeah... nice," she drawls. "That's *quite* a colour. But you can't taste the colour pink, my friend. You want to try one of these perfume flowers. I'm telling you! My Lilac, she may be a plain old shrub, but nothing makes honey quite like it!"

ASK THE CLASS: Is that strange that the two older siblings both prefer different flowers?

LOVE

Read this story aloud to the group, using the prompt questions to encourage active listening.

PART 3

Buzz settles back into the crack in the stone wall to watch Pedro, Lupita and the other older bees enjoying the festival. The little bee isn't sure where to start. *Will I ever make honey? Will any flower want me?*

Buzz flies toward a fancy Rose and gives it the tiniest prod with his wing. His stomach churns with worry. It looks so... purple. But the Rose sways away in the breeze. He zooms off, embarrassed, pretending nothing happened. *It didn't smell right anyway*, Buzz tells himself. That's when he catches sight of something right at the other end of the garden. A shy Daisy hidden by a statue. Its tiny white petals are waving in the wind. Could they be waving at him? Buzz's body floods with a warm feeling. His wings carry him over before he can stop them.

ASK THE CLASS: Have you ever had a "gut feeling" when you know how you feel, but you can't explain why?

PART 4

Buzz comes back the next morning, and the next after that. Every day of summer, the bee chooses the Daisy. And every day, the Daisy opens its petals to the bee. Between them, they make a new and wonderful honey that tastes like nothing else on earth. He'll never persuade Pedro, but to Buzz, it's the most wonderful flavour in the world.

ASK THE CLASS: What happens if they ever stop choosing each other? Will the bee or the flower die?

LOVE

The story has a message about love. Write what each part of the story might stand for.

This part of the story:

Is like:

This part of the story		Is like
HONEY	=	*Love*
THE BEES AND THE FLOWERS	=	_____ _____ _____
WHAT EACH BEE LIKES ABOUT ITS FLOWER (COLOURS, SMELLS)	=	_____ _____ _____
THE FLOWER TURNING AWAY FROM THE BEE OR THE BEE BUZZING OFF	=	_____ _____ _____
RETURNING TO THE SAME FLOWER EVERY DAY	=	_____ _____ _____

LOVE

This part of the story:		**Is like:**
HONEY	=	*Love*
THE BEES AND THE FLOWERS	=	*People looking for love*
WHAT EACH BEE PREFERS IN A FLOWER (COLOURS, SMELLS)	=	*What someone finds attractive in other people*
THE FLOWER TURNING AWAY FROM THE BEE OR THE BEE BUZZING OFF	=	*When someone doesn't return another person's romantic feelings*
RETURNING TO THE SAME FLOWER EVERY DAY	=	*Being in a romantic relationship*

LEARNING POINT

WHAT CAN WE SAY ABOUT LOVE?

- When two people come together and it feels right, something special is made between them.
- They continue to choose each other as long as it works for both.

How is honey like love? Match up the story cards (1–5) with the explanation cards (A–E).

STORY CARDS

EXPLANATION CARDS

	Story		Explanation
1	When a bee and a flower come together, **SOMETHING SPECIAL IS MADE.**	A	Bees and flowers are helping each other when honey is created. There's a word for that: "mutual." Love in human relationships should feel mutual (two people understanding and helping each other). If it doesn't, it's probably not right.
2	Honeymaking **HAPPENS NATURALLY** (it's part of nature).	B	A bee doesn't always have to choose the same flower. And sometimes, human relationships come to a natural end and people move on. Both the bee and the flower will be ok if that happens. They will probably even find new partners one day.
3	The way honey is made is **MUTUAL** (it is good for both bee and flower).	C	Out of the partnership between a bee and a flower, something miraculous and even mysterious is created. How does it work? Like love, there's no simple way to describe it. Love is very complex and difficult to explain; that's why a lot of art has been created and written about it.
4	The bee and the flower are **ATTRACTED** to each other.	D	Being attracted to something means being drawn toward it without necessarily being able to explain why (like a bee's instinct to find a flower). If one person feels that attraction for a short time we can call it a crush. If the feeling is mutual (both people feel it) and it grows into something strong, we call it love.
5	Bees and flowers are **NOT NECESSARILY PAIRED FOREVER,** and that's ok.	E	A flower doesn't "decide" to make nectar, and a bee feels its way there without thinking; these things happen naturally. Just like that love is a feeling, not a decision. That's why people say *only your heart can decide.* It can't be forced or rushed, but it can happen for everyone.

1 matches with ___   3 matches with ___   5 matches with ___

2 matches with ___   4 matches with ___

| LOVE |
|

EXTENSION ACTIVITIES

 Watch a video on how honey is made and then create a diagram or flowchart that lays out the steps. The diagram should show what the bee *and* the flower get from the partnership. Discuss what those benefits might be in a human romantic relationship.

 Read some love poems (try "Yours" by Daniel Hoffman, "Scaffolding" by Seamus Heaney, and "Love Poem with Apologies for My Appearance" by Ada Limón). In groups, discuss which one you think best describes what love is. Have a vote afterward.

 Think of a famous "dream team" in which two people have come together to do or create something wonderful. Get together in pairs to discuss what each gets from the other.

ANSWERS for the card matching activity

1 matches with C
2 matches with E
3 matches with A
4 matches with D
5 matches with B

TEACHING NOTES

- **Group management:** Some children will already be interested in "dating" or they may have crushes on others within their peer group. If you are aware of this, then manage how groups of learners are formed for the activity to avoid embarrassment or teasing.
- **Children's home circumstances:** Be mindful of children whose parents are experiencing break-ups, divorce or new relationships. It can be helpful to use the metaphor to emphasise that love is not always mutual or that people grow apart, but new love can be found.

14 How a baby is made
Reproduction

Sc
Science

S
Sex
education

LEARNING POINTS	KEYWORDS
Human reproduction is when a baby is made. The most common way for the egg and sperm to meet is when a female and a male have sex. This is when the couple enjoy each other's bodies in a sexual way. The penis goes into the vagina and semen (sperm and fluid) is released from the penis and travels through the vagina into the womb. If an egg has been recently released from an ovary, the sperm will meet it in the fallopian tube. This is called conception and starts the pregnancy. The baby will develop until it is ready to be born. If a people cannot conceive a baby through sex, then there are other ways to help a sperm and egg meet. Babies need love, nurturing, safety and lots of care to thrive and grow. All babies are beautiful, no matter how they are made or how they come into a family.	Human life cycle Menstrual cycle Reproduction Eggs (ovum) Sperm Womb (uterus) Fallopian tube Penis Vagina Sex Pregnancy Fertility treatment Gestation Birth Babies Unique Family Love Nurture Safety Information Support Help

DOI: 10.4324/9781003391654-17

Read this story aloud to the group, using the prompt questions to encourage active listening.

PART 1

Carlos's new life had a colour, and the colour was grey. The endless tarmac, the huge building that the grown-ups called their "temporary accommodation," and even the sky over this cold country: all grey.

Home had been a colourful place. The day they'd had to leave Mexico, Carlos had been with his granny – his *abuela* – in their big sunny lime grove, planting flowers up against the pink walls. There had been a bit of a rush that day. Carlos only had time to bring two things to his grey new country: the winter coat he had thrown on, and the half-empty packet of Mexican sunflower seeds he had shoved into its pocket. They even had to leave Abuela behind.

Carlos and his sister Ana didn't have a new school yet, so they spent most days chasing pigeons or stalking squirrels around by the bins. That's where he found the six stacked flowerpots – cracked but usable – that gave him an idea.

ASK THE CLASS: What do you think is Carlos's idea?

PART 2

A week later, Ana and Carlos were watering the pots on the windowsill of their dark kitchen. They were mostly empty, with one or two sad, yellowing little sprouts. "I don't think these will grow in this country," said Ana. "They have their own sunflowers here."

Carlos turned to her and carefully pronounced a single English word: *nonsense*. He had learned it before they even left Mexico, from a peaceful, upbeat English language show that he used to watch with Abuela, called *Bumper Crop*. "When seed meets soil, a flower is made," he said, quoting the presenter of *Bumper Crop*. Seed and soil – *simple* – but there was one other thing missing. He marched out to the main entrance and put the pots outside on the bright doorstep of the apartment building.

ASK THE CLASS: Why didn't the seeds grow in their dark kitchen?

HOW A BABY IS MADE

Read this story aloud to the group, using the prompt questions to encourage active listening.

PART 3

Another week later, Ana and Carlos were bending over the scattered remains of the six pots on the doorstep of the building. Soil was spread everywhere, leaving big brown footprints all around. Most of the seedlings were lying, dried and browning, on the ground. Carlos found one with its tiny stalk cut in half by the rim of an upturned pot; it looked like a broken neck. Just one of the six remained upright. It had been tucked slightly out of the way, and its strong, green stalk was still reaching for the sun.

ASK THE CLASS: What else does Carlos discover that a seed needs to grow, apart from soil, water and light?

PART 4

Inside a beautiful pink house in Mexico, an old lady leans close to her old TV set. Are her eyes deceiving her, or is that her grandson Carlos standing next to the presenter of *Bumper Crop*?

"Next up: we heard from Carlos, aged 9, to say that he was having a spot of bother with his Mexican sunflowers. So, we got in touch to help." Carlos is on screen, standing in a magnificent greenhouse outside a tall, grey apartment block, surrounded by a forest of bright orange flowers.

"I found out that seeds and soil aren't all you need. This variety likes a bit of peace and quiet and plenty of sunshine," Carlos says into the microphone. "The sun in the sky today: that's the same sun that is shining down upon my Abuela. It takes care of both of our gardens."

ASK THE CLASS: Was it true the flowers could only grow in Mexico?

SUPPORT MATERIAL

HOW A BABY IS MADE

The story has a message about how a baby is made. Write what each part of the story might stand for.

This part of the story: **Is like:**

GROWING A SUNFLOWER = *Growing a baby*

WHEN A SEED AND SOME SOIL ARE BROUGHT TOGETHER = _____ _____ _____

THE MANY DIFFERENT PLACES YOU CAN GROW A SUNFLOWER = _____ _____ _____

SUNSHINE = _____ _____ _____

SMALL DIFFERENCES IN EACH SUNFLOWER, BUT ALL ARE BEAUTIFUL = _____ _____ _____

HOW A BABY IS MADE

This part of the story:		**Is like:**
GROWING A SUNFLOWER	=	*Growing a baby*
WHEN A SEED AND SOME SOIL ARE BROUGHT TOGETHER	=	*When an egg (ovum) and sperm meet inside a human body*
THE MANY DIFFERENT PLACES YOU CAN GROW A SUNFLOWER	=	*Different ways to bring a baby into the world*
SUNSHINE	=	*The love and support a child needs while growing up*
SMALL DIFFERENCES IN EACH SUNFLOWER, BUT ALL ARE BEAUTIFUL	=	*Small differences in each baby, but all are beautiful!*

LEARNING POINT

WHAT CAN WE SAY ABOUT HOW A BABY IS MADE?

- You need two basic things to come together, but that can happen in several different ways.
- They need a safe place to grow and plenty of love.

How is a sunflower like a baby? Match up the story cards (1–5) with the explanation cards (A–E).

STORY CARDS

EXPLANATION CARDS

1	**To grow a sunflower, you need TWO THINGS TO COME TOGETHER.**	A	A baby can be made when a man and woman have sex and their sperm and egg come together inside the woman's womb. Or scientists can help a baby to be created from sperm and egg outside the body, for example, in a test tube. It's just like a sunflower: you can grow one in the greenhouse, in the ground or on a windowsill.
2	**There are DIFFERENT WAYS to bring a sunflower into the world.**	B	Without plenty of sunshine, no healthy plant could grow. That sunshine is like love for humans. Children need an environment with plenty of love and care to make them grow healthy and happy. But that love can come in many different forms and from many different caring adults.
3	**All sunflowers NEED SUNSHINE TO THRIVE.**	C	Plants are fragile at first; they need shelter and ready-made food from inside their seed until they grow strong enough to survive above the soil. In the same way, human babies grow for 9 months inside the womb (uterus), where it is safe and warm, and they are fed through a tube straight from the woman's body.
4	**Sunflowers NEED A SAFE PLACE TO GROW until they can make it on their own.**	D	You might think there is only one type of sunflower, but that is just the kind that you are used to seeing. In fact, they come in all shapes, sizes and colours. In just the same way, all babies are unique. Like all living things, each one grows in a slightly different way, and all are beautiful.
5	**Sunflowers each come out LOOKING DIFFERENT, BUT ALL ARE BEAUTIFUL.**	E	You need to put two things together inside a container to grow a sunflower: a seed and some soil. Babies also grow when two ingredients come together: two types of human cells called a sperm and an egg (ovum). When that happens, and the egg is "fertilised," it starts growing into a baby.

1 matches with ___   3 matches with ___   5 matches with ___

2 matches with ___   4 matches with ___

HOW A BABY IS MADE

EXTENSION ACTIVITIES

 Write a list of things a young plant needs to grow and thrive. Write a second list of things a young baby needs to survive and grow. How many are similar?

 Draw a picture of a small plant, including the seed it has grown from. Label your drawing with the words POT, SOIL, SEED, PLANT, SUN. Imagine the flower is a human baby. Write alternative labels based on the metaphor explored in Carlos's story.

 Research seeds on the internet or in a book. On one piece of paper, draw a large, "blown up" version of any seed you have discovered. On another, draw the plant it can become. Muddle up everyone's pictures and play a game in groups to match the seeds with the plants. Discuss what the pictures would look like for human reproduction.

ANSWERS for the card matching activity

1 matches with E

2 matches with A

3 matches with B

4 matches with C

5 matches with D

TEACHING NOTES

- **Diversity:** Become familiar with the diverse cultural backgrounds represented within the classroom. These may affect how much the children learn at home about how a baby is made. Likewise, children with older siblings may know more about sex than others. Do all the children feel visible and represented in a positive and inclusive way during the session?

- **Questions about sex:** Children may ask questions about sex and sexual practices. Consult your RSHE policy so that you know how sex education is defined and the guidance in place for dealing with children's questions. You could invite children to pose their questions anonymously in a Question Box and prep your answers for a dedicated Q&A session.

- **Safeguarding:** Follow your setting's Child Protection and Safeguarding policies and speak with the Designated Safeguarding Lead regarding **any** concerns about a child's welfare: disclosure or indicators of abuse, neglect or exploitation. Signpost to sources of support and help.

15 When people have sex
Sexual activity

R
Relationships education

S
Sex education

LEARNING POINTS	KEYWORDS
Sex is when people touch each other's private body parts, and it feels good. People decide to have sex to share love and affection; some like to do it for fun and sometimes it is because they want to have a baby. People have to feel ready and be old enough and mature enough to have sex. In the UK you have to be 16 before you're legally able to make the decision to have sex. Lots of people wait till they are older than 16 and not everybody wants to have sex. In some cultures or religions, it is important to be married before you have sex. People should never be pressured into having sex or made to feel bad because they don't want to. Everybody gets to decide for themselves.	Sex Private body parts Love and affection Mutual respect Boundaries Consent Maturity Readiness Choice Trust Responsibility Communication Safety Contraception Information Support Help

DOI: 10.4324/9781003391654-18

WHEN PEOPLE HAVE SEX

Read this story aloud to the group, using the prompt questions to encourage active listening.

PART 1

Two people decide to cycle around the world. They don't have anywhere in particular to be, they just want to. Perhaps it's because they're proud citizens of the cycling capital of the world: a flat, friendly country in northern Europe, where no other mode of transport exists.

The sun is shining, as it always does, when the pair decides they are ready. They have lovely new mountain bikes, and they know how to ride them.

Their parents gather to wave them off. As the pair cycle off, almost out of earshot, the oldest and greyest amongst the parents calls: "come back if the sun stops shining!"

They breeze along the wide cycle paths of Amsterdam. They dawdle along the banks of the Danube and through the greenest parts of Europe. They whizz across the great plains of Russia. All the while, the sun shines.

ASK THE CLASS: Who would want to go for a bike ride in the sunshine? Who would want to go in the pouring rain?

PART 2

The pair reach the city of Kathmandu. Here, the landscape is hilly. They can still ride, but they are tested like never before.

A loud metal machine on big thick wheels zooms past them. It spews out thick smoke. "A truck!" they shout at each other. Then another, a little smaller, then another, until the machines have almost completely taken over the road.

That's when the cyclists feel the first drop of rain. It begins to patter down. Soon, it's running down their bodies in rivers, blinding their eyes and freezing up their legs.

One shouts back at the other, asking whether they should carry on or stop. But at that moment, they clip one another's wheels. "Stay left!" one yells through the storm at the other, "You're pushing me into those cars!"

ASK THE CLASS: What are some things that can go wrong on a bike trip?

WHEN PEOPLE HAVE SEX

Read this story aloud to the group, using the prompt questions to encourage active listening.

PART 3

Feeling defeated, the pair dismount their bikes at the side of the road, and it's at that moment that they remember that each has a package in their basket: a parting gift from their parents. From one basket, out come a pair of bike helmets. "That should do the trick," says one, unconvincingly. "It'll keep us safe, at least." The other adds, with a gloomy tone. "It might keep some of the rain off, too." Both are still shivering.

From the second basket come a pair of bells and a pair of lights: "We can make ourselves seen and heard, now," they say to each other, bracingly. "So at least we won't get knocked off, I suppose."

ASK THE CLASS: Are they still enjoying their bike trip?

PART 4

They look at each other, steeling themselves to get back on the bikes, when one sees the note at the bottom of their basket, kept dry by the packages. "Come back if the sun stops shining," it says, in spidery writing.

One of the cyclists bursts into tears. They like cycling. Why aren't they having fun? They look around them, and they realise that nobody's cycling here. Maybe in some places, some climates, some landscapes, it's not fun, at least not all the time? Maybe, they say to each other, they'll catch a train for the next bit.

ASK THE CLASS: What other activities are only fun in certain circumstances?

WHEN PEOPLE HAVE SEX

The story has a message about sex. Write what each part of the story might stand for.

This part of the story:

Is like:

SHARING A BIKE TRIP = *Having sex with someone*

SAFETY EQUIPMENT LIKE HELMETS AND LIGHTS = _____

PLACES THAT AREN'T GOOD FOR CYCLING = _____

WHEN IT'S SUNNY AND FLAT = _____

CHOOSING TO TAKE THE TRAIN FOR THE NEXT BIT = _____

WHEN PEOPLE HAVE SEX

This part of the story:		Is like:
SHARING A BIKE TRIP	=	*Having sex with someone*
SAFETY EQUIPMENT LIKE HELMETS AND LIGHTS	=	*Physical and mental tools to stay safe when having sex*
PLACES THAT AREN'T GOOD FOR CYCLING	=	*Circumstances or contexts when it's not a good idea to have sex*
WHEN IT'S SUNNY AND FLAT	=	*When it feels right, e.g., if you love and trust each other*
CHOOSING TO TAKE THE TRAIN FOR THE NEXT BIT	=	*Choosing not to have sex when it doesn't feel right for both people*

LEARNING POINT

WHAT CAN WE SAY ABOUT HAVING SEX?

- It is only a good idea when both people are ready, and everything is in place to enjoy it safely.
- No one should be pressured into doing it, and people can change their minds at any time.

137

How is a bike trip like choosing to have sex? Match up the story cards (1–5) with the explanation cards (A–E).

STORY CARDS

EXPLANATION CARDS

1	A bike trip is FOR FUN and sometimes also for a PRACTICAL PURPOSE.	A

You probably wouldn't choose to go cycling in the pouring rain; it's nicest in the sunshine. And when people choose to have sex, the circumstances (and context) need to be right – usually in a loving relationship and when your culture believes it's ok. Not everyone wants to have sex at the same age or stage of life.

2	You need to BE RESPONSIBLE AND FEEL READY to go on a bike trip.	B

Everyone knows you have to wear a helmet on a bike trip and use a bell, a light and hand signals to communicate with fellow road users. It's the same with sex: there are things you can use to keep you safe (e.g., contraception, which are ways to avoid pregnancy and passing on infections). There are mental and emotional tools too, such as when sexual partners use good communication to stay in touch with each other's feelings.

3	There are GOOD AND BAD TIMES to go on a bike trip.	C

Cycling comes with a responsibility to the other people on the road. And people who have sex also need to take care of each other's bodies and feelings. That's why both people need to be ready, just like riding a bike. You need to feel that you are old enough to cope if it doesn't go how you want it to.

4	There are important TOOLS AND EQUIPMENT to make a bike trip fun and safe.	D

Someone should only go on a bike trip if they want to, and it feels right. It's the same for having sex (when people touch each other's private body parts in ways that feel good). Of course, cycling can also be a useful way to get from A to B. There is another reason for having sex, too: to make a baby.

5	YOU CAN STOP AND GET OFF on a bike trip at any time.	E

On a bike trip, you could stop and get off your bike any time you like, even if you hadn't reached your destination or you thought your fellow cyclist was having fun. Sex is also something that needs to stop unless both people are safe and enjoying themselves.

1 matches with ___   3 matches with ___   5 matches with ___

2 matches with ___   4 matches with ___

WHEN PEOPLE HAVE SEX

EXTENSION ACTIVITIES

Think about all the different things people have to consider before they decide to have sex. Apart from being old enough and mature enough, what would be important to you? Write down a list and compare it with others'. Do you have things in common, or do other people have values different from yours?

Cut out and glue pictures from magazines to make a collage representing all the different views and values that surround sex in our society (for example wedding pictures, how advertising uses references to sex, how people express their attraction to others, etc.).

On a small piece of paper, write the age at which you think most people are ready to have sex. Gather the whole group's responses, anonymously, and count them up. Create a graph to represent the range of opinions. Discuss how else, apart from age, someone could decide whether they are ready to have sex.

ANSWERS for the card matching activity

1 matches with D

2 matches with C

3 matches with A

4 matches with B

5 matches with E

TEACHING NOTES

- **Diversity:** Become familiar with the diverse cultural backgrounds represented within the classroom. These may affect how much the children learn at home about sexual relationships. Likewise, children with older siblings may know more about sex than others. Perhaps there are differing views and values on sex or sex before marriage. Do all the children feel visible and represented in a positive and inclusive way during the session?

- **Questions about sex:** Children may ask questions about sex to which the answers may be defined as sex education. Check how your setting's RSHE policy defines sex education and the guidance in place for dealing with children's questions. An anonymous Question Box can help you manage the session.

- **Safeguarding:** Follow your setting's Child Protection and Safeguarding policies and speak with the Designated Safeguarding Lead regarding **any** concerns about a child's welfare: disclosure or indicators of abuse, neglect or exploitation. Signpost to sources of support and help.

9781032489650

T - #0035 - 101123 - C148 - 297/210/7 - SB - 9781032489650 - Gloss Lamination